This

belongs To:
Ruben Goitia
Grade 1
St. Patricks School

Illustrators Mike Atkinson, Jim Dugdale,
Ron Jobson and Roger Payne

Compiled and designed for
World International Publishing Ltd.
by Michael W. Dempsey,
27 John Adam Street,
London WC2.

The CHILDREN'S
FIRST GEOGRAPHY
ENCYCLOPEDIA

Michael W. Dempsey and Ian James

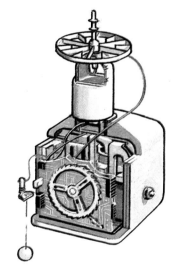

Exeter Books

NEW YORK

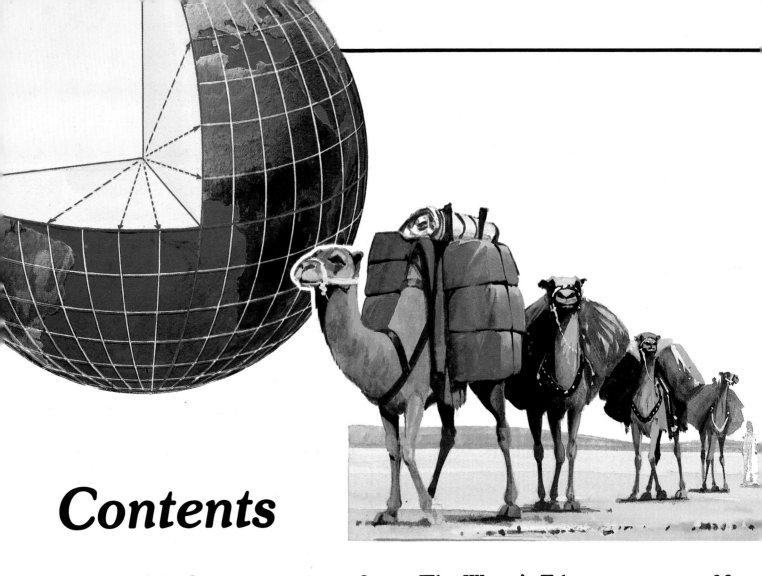

Contents

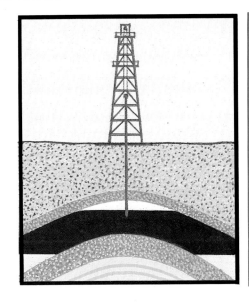
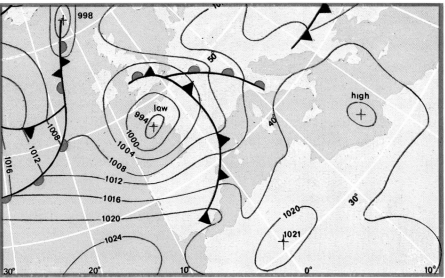

The Earth in Space

Our Earth is like a giant spaceship and we are space travelers. The Earth moves in three ways. First, it spins on its axis, making one turn in 24 hours. Second, it rotates around the Sun at an average speed of 65,991 mph. It takes 365 days, 48 minutes and 46 seconds, or one *solar year*, to complete one orbit. Because this is longer than our 365-day *calendar year*, we have leap years of 366 days to stop the solar and calendar years getting out of step.

The Earth also moves with the Sun, the planets and the other bodies that form the Solar System around the Milky Way galaxy. It takes about 200 million years to complete one circuit around the galaxy.

Looking After Planet Earth

Spaceship Earth has all the resources we need and its resources are constantly but slowly renewed. The study of planet Earth is extremely important. Only by understanding our Earth will we be able to ensure that it remains a good home for future generations.

Right: The Earth rotates on its axis, the imaginary line joining the North Pole, the center of the Earth and the South Pole. At the equator, where the speed of rotation is greatest, the Earth is spinning at a speed of 1043 mph. The speed of rotation decreases away from the equator towards the poles. When a place on Earth faces the Sun, it enjoys daylight. When that same place turns away from the Sun, it is night. The Earth takes 23 hours, 56 minutes and 4 seconds to complete one full turn on its axis. This is the *sidereal day*. But while the Earth is spinning on its axis, it is also moving forward on its 365-day orbit around the Sun. Hence, the time taken for a point on Earth to face the Sun on two successive occasions is slightly longer than the sidereal day. In fact, the Earth must turn 1/365th more than one complete rotation before the point exactly faces the Sun. The time taken for this extra turn gives the *mean solar day* a length of 24 hours. The hours of daylight vary throughout the year.

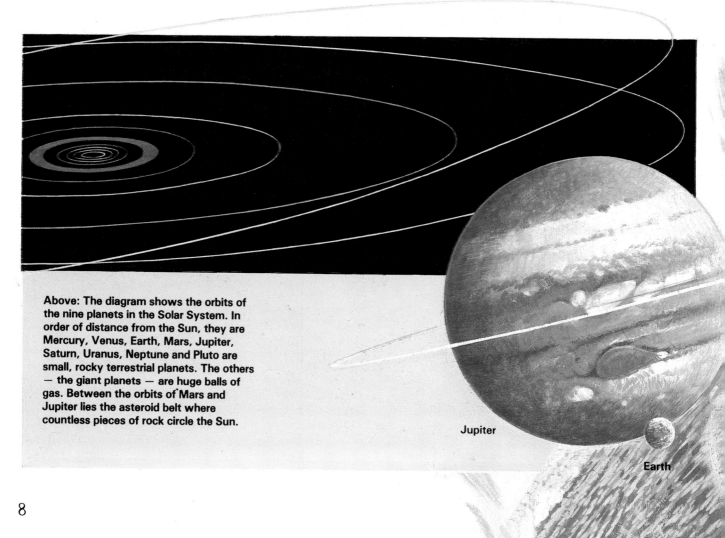

Above: The diagram shows the orbits of the nine planets in the Solar System. In order of distance from the Sun, they are Mercury, Venus, Earth, Mars, Jupiter, Saturn, Uranus, Neptune and Pluto are small, rocky terrestrial planets. The others — the giant planets — are huge balls of gas. Between the orbits of Mars and Jupiter lies the asteroid belt where countless pieces of rock circle the Sun.

Jupiter

Earth

Evening

Sun's rays

Midnight

Midday

Morning

Sun's rays

Below: The Sun measures 870,000 miles across. It is 109 times as big as the Earth and nearly 10 times the size of the planet Jupiter – the largest planet. The Sun has an average surface temperature of 6000°C. It bakes the surfaces of Mercury and Venus. But the average surface temperature on Earth is 22°C. On Jupiter, however, the surface temperature is down to −150°C.

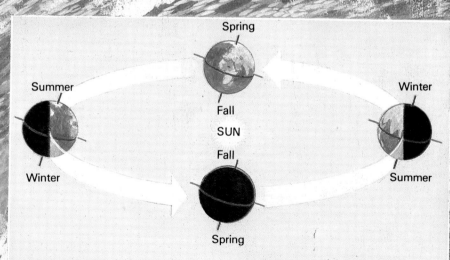

Spring

Fall

Summer

SUN

Winter

Winter

Fall

Summer

Spring

Above: Because the Earth's axis is tilted by 23½ degrees as it orbits the Sun, the northern and southern hemispheres lean towards and away from the Sun, causing seasons. On June 21, the summer solstice, the northern hemisphere leans towards the Sun to its greatest extent. On September 23, the autumn equinox, the Sun is overhead at the equator and the length of day and night is equal everywhere in the world. The southern hemisphere then tilts towards the Sun until December 23, the winter solstice, which is followed by the spring equinox on March 21. (The seasons are reversed south of the equator.)

Birth of the Earth

Most scientists now agree that the Earth was formed from a cloud of gas and dust. This cloud was drifting through space about 5000 million years ago. Gradually, more and more particles were drawn to the center by gravity. There, about 4600 million years ago, they formed a star, the Sun. The material left over formed the planets, moons and other bodies that make up the Solar System.

Above: The Earth is made up of three parts. The thin crust varies between 40 miles thick under the highest mountains to 3 miles thick under the oceans. Beneath the crust is the denser (heavier) mantle. The mantle is about 1800 miles thick. It encloses the extremely dense core, which measures about 4300 miles across. The inner core is solid, but the outer core is probably liquid.

The Earth's Early History

The youthful Earth was probably a huge ball of gas, rather like Jupiter or Saturn. But eventually, because of gravity, heavier elements, notably iron, sank towards the center, forming a dense core, while lighter elements stayed near the surface. As a result, the Earth now has a very dense (heavy) core, made up largely of iron and nickel, a dense mantle and a relatively light crust.

The Earth slowly shrank into the rocky planet we know today. At first, the surface was hot and molten. Geologists have not found any rocks much older than about 3800 million years, although the Earth itself is about 4550 million years old. Rocks formed in the first 700 million years were probably all broken up and remelted.

The Earth's first atmosphere was poisonous, but it contained water vapor released from the rocks by volcanoes. It contained little oxygen, the gas we need to breathe. The oxygen content began to increase about 1900 million years ago, when oxygen-producing plants first developed.

Below: For many millions of years after its formation, the Earth's surface must have been blazing hot. Constant volcanic activity released gas and water vapor from the rocks inside the Earth. The gases formed a primitive and poisonous atmosphere. Later on, when the surface started to cool, there were great thunderstorms. Rain started to fill up hollows in the early crust. It was perhaps in these warm pools that the first living things, bacteria, appeared.

THE EARTH'S DIMENSIONS

DIAMETER: The equatorial diameter is 7927 miles, but the polar diameter is shorter, 7900 miles.

CIRCUMFERENCE: The equatorial circumference (the distance around the equator) is 24,902 miles. But if you travel around the Earth via the poles (the polar circumference), the distance is only 24,860 miles.

AREA: The Earth has an area of 197,272,000 sq. miles.

LAND AND SEA: The oceans cover nearly 71 per cent of the Earth's surface.

The Hidden Past

Fossils are evidence found in rocks of animals and plants which once lived on Earth. They range from animal footprints to animal bones, plants turned to stone and insects preserved in amber.

Why Fossils are Important

Fossils occur in rocks all over the world. Because rock layers are folded and pushed upwards, fossils of seashells are found even at the tops of mountains. The study of fossils helps geologists to date rocks. It also helps us to understand the evolution of plants and animals throughout Earth history.

The pictures above show how a fossil is formed. When an animal dies (1), it must be buried quickly in underwater sediments. The flesh soon decays, but the bones survive (2).

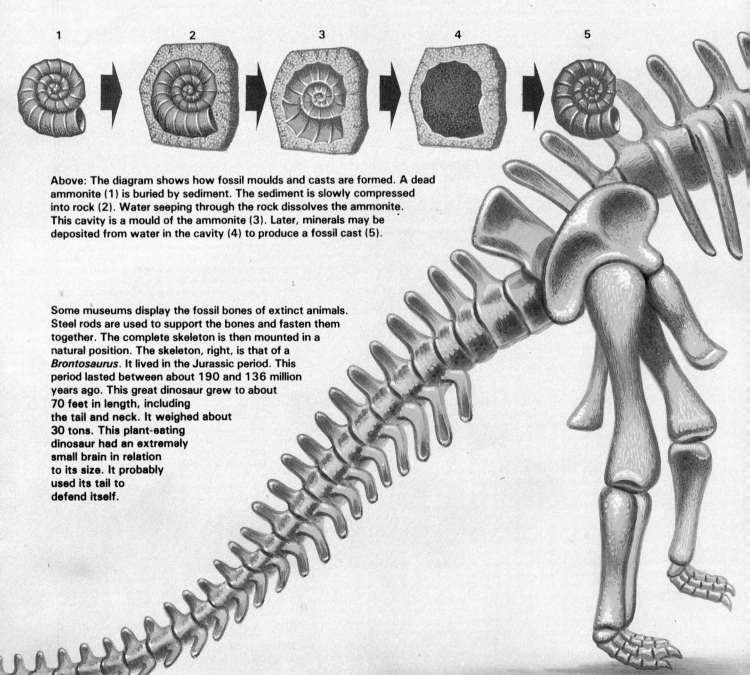

Above: The diagram shows how fossil moulds and casts are formed. A dead ammonite (1) is buried by sediment. The sediment is slowly compressed into rock (2). Water seeping through the rock dissolves the ammonite. This cavity is a mould of the ammonite (3). Later, minerals may be deposited from water in the cavity (4) to produce a fossil cast (5).

Some museums display the fossil bones of extinct animals. Steel rods are used to support the bones and fasten them together. The complete skeleton is then mounted in a natural position. The skeleton, right, is that of a *Brontosaurus*. It lived in the Jurassic period. This period lasted between about 190 and 136 million years ago. This great dinosaur grew to about 70 feet in length, including the tail and neck. It weighed about 30 tons. This plant-eating dinosaur had an extremely small brain in relation to its size. It probably used its tail to defend itself.

2

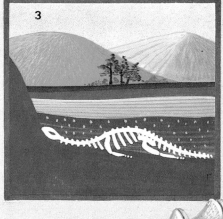

3

4

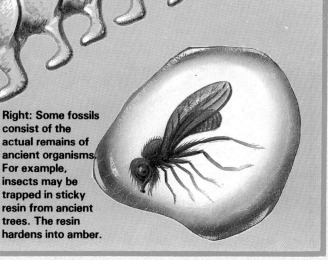

The sediments are pressed into hard rock. Minerals penetrate the buried bones, turning them into stone (3). Millions of years later, the rocks are raised up and worn down, revealing the fossil (4).

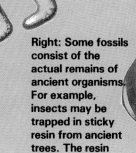

Right: Some fossils consist of the actual remains of ancient organisms. For example, insects may be trapped in sticky resin from ancient trees. The resin hardens into amber.

A person compared in size with Brontosaurus

The Formation of Fossils

For fossils to form, the remains of animals and plants must be buried quickly. Otherwise, they would rot on the surface. Burial usually takes place in the mud, silt and sand on sea, lake and river beds. After burial, the flesh of a dead animal usually decays. Hard parts, such as bones and shells, are preserved. The sediments are gradually turned into solid rock. Water seeping through the rock often deposits minerals in the pores of bones and shells, slowly turning them into stone. Sometimes, every tiny molecule of a buried log is replaced by minerals. This process forms *petrified* logs. Leaves preserved in rocks sometimes form thin films of carbon which show the shape of the leaf.

Other fossils are moulds or casts of the original hard parts (see the diagrams on the facing page). A few fossils include the actual bodies of animals, such as woolly mammoths which lived 30,000 years ago. These have been preserved in the frozen ground of Siberia. But such fossils are extremely rare.

Ages of the Earth

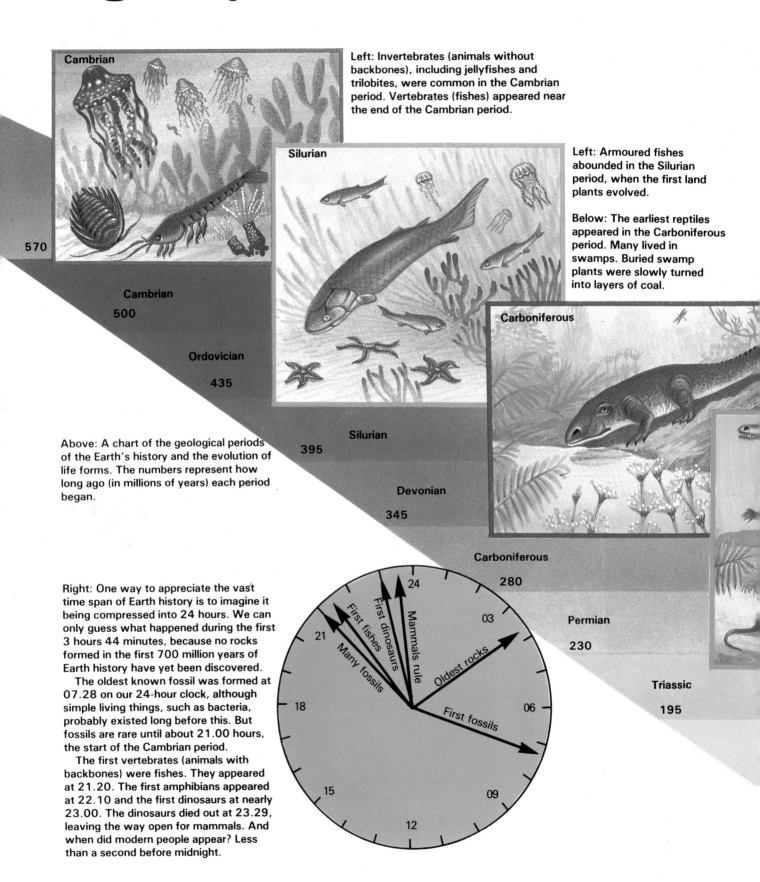

Cambrian

570

500

Left: Invertebrates (animals without backbones), including jellyfishes and trilobites, were common in the Cambrian period. Vertebrates (fishes) appeared near the end of the Cambrian period.

Silurian

Left: Armoured fishes abounded in the Silurian period, when the first land plants evolved.

Below: The earliest reptiles appeared in the Carboniferous period. Many lived in swamps. Buried swamp plants were slowly turned into layers of coal.

Carboniferous

Cambrian
500

Ordovician
435

Silurian
395

Devonian
345

Carboniferous
280

Permian
230

Triassic
195

Above: A chart of the geological periods of the Earth's history and the evolution of life forms. The numbers represent how long ago (in millions of years) each period began.

Right: One way to appreciate the vast time span of Earth history is to imagine it being compressed into 24 hours. We can only guess what happened during the first 3 hours 44 minutes, because no rocks formed in the first 700 million years of Earth history have yet been discovered.

The oldest known fossil was formed at 07.28 on our 24-hour clock, although simple living things, such as bacteria, probably existed long before this. But fossils are rare until about 21.00 hours, the start of the Cambrian period.

The first vertebrates (animals with backbones) were fishes. They appeared at 21.20. The first amphibians appeared at 22.10 and the first dinosaurs at nearly 23.00. The dinosaurs died out at 23.29, leaving the way open for mammals. And when did modern people appear? Less than a second before midnight.

Many fossils
First fishes
First dinosaurs
Mammals rule
Oldest rocks
First fossils

24
03
06
09
12
15
18
21

Dating Rocks

The study of fossils made possible the fixing of the relative ages of rocks. And in the early 20th century, the discovery of radioactivity enabled scientists to fix the absolute ages of rocks. This is because some rocks contain bits of radioactive material which decays, or breaks down, at a fixed rate. Therefore, when scientists measure the proportion of a radioactive substance that has decayed, they can establish its age.

Eras and Periods

The last 570 million years are divided into the Palaeozoic (ancient life), Mesozoic (middle life) and Cenozoic (recent life) eras.

The Palaeozoic era (570-230 million years ago) is divided into six periods, although US geologists divide the Carboniferous period into two: the Mississippian and Pennsylvanian periods. The first period of the Palaeozoic era is the Cambrian. Cambrian rocks are rich in fossils. But in Precambrian rocks, formed before the Cambrian period began, fossils are rare. The Palaeozoic era saw the appearance of the first vertebrates (fishes), amphibians and reptiles.

The Mesozoic era (230-65 million years ago), contains three periods. It saw the rise of reptiles, including huge dinosaurs. Most reptiles became extinct at the end of the era.

The Cenozoic era in the last 65 million years saw the rise of mammals. This era contains two periods: the Tertiary and the Quaternary. Mighty mountain ranges such as the Alps and Himalayas were born during this era.

Above: The British Isles would look like this if the sea level rose or if the land sank by only 200 feet. The land and sea have changed many times throughout Earth history.

Left: The first dinosaurs appeared in the Triassic period. The first mammals also evolved at this time.

Below left: The Jurassic period saw the emergence of such dinosaurs as *Brontosaurus* and *Stegosaurus*. There were flying reptiles, called Pterosaurs, and the first bird, *Archaeopteryx*.

Below: The Tertiary and Quaternary periods were dominated by mammals, such as giant ground sloths, huge grazing animals, sabre-toothed tigers and many birds. Primates date back 60 million years. Modern people (who are primates) appeared about 50,000 years ago.

Triassic

Jurassic

Tertiary

Jurassic

Cretaceous

65

Tertiary

1.8

Quaternary

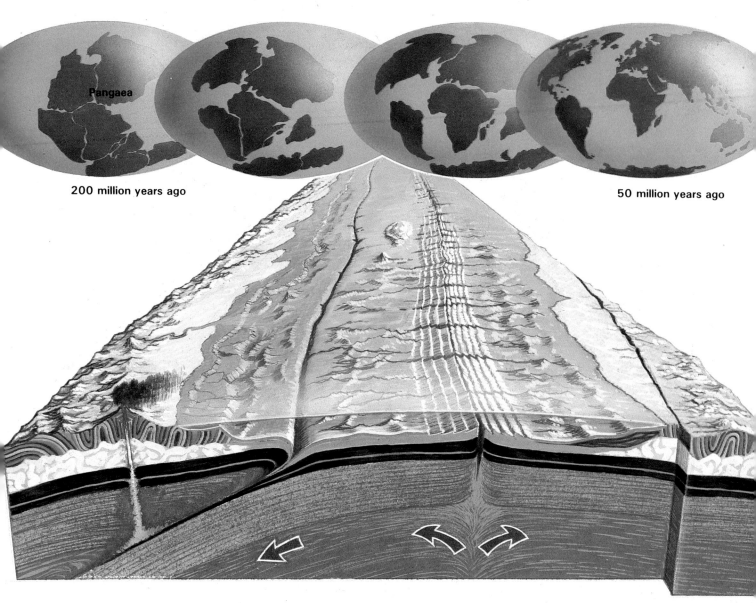

Pangaea

200 million years ago

50 million years ago

The Earth Beneath

Look at a map of the Atlantic Ocean. You will see that North and South America look as though they would fit together with Europe and Africa, like pieces in a jigsaw. About 70 years ago, some scientists suggested that the continents were once joined together.

A German, Alfred Wegener (1880-1930), found similar rock structures on the edges of the facing continents. Fossils of the same land animals, which lived around 200 million years ago, were dug up in South America and Africa. How did they get there? They could not have swum the ocean. Wegener was convinced that the continents had been joined together 200 million years ago. But how do continents move?

Top: the maps show how the world has changed over the last 200 million years.

Above: The diagram shows an ocean ridge rising from the sea floor. In the center of these ridges are valleys. These valleys are the edges of plates. Semi-molten material in the upper mantle is rising beneath the ridges. Under the plates it divides and flows sideways, pulling the plates apart. As the plates move, molten material wells up to fill the gap. It hardens into new crustal rock.

Along the deep ocean trenches, the fluid material sinks dowards and one plate is pushed beneath another. The diagram shows plates moving apart and plates colliding. Other plates move alongside each other. Such plates are separated by cracks called transform faults.

16

THE EARTH'S CHANGING FACE

A space traveler passing the Earth 200 million years ago would have seen one large landmass and one vast blue ocean. But around 135 million years ago, the landmass, called Pangaea, had started to break up and the pieces were slowly drifting apart. The modern oceans were created between them. Some plates were large. Others, like the one carrying what is now India, were smaller. The Indian plate had been attached to Africa. But around 50 million years ago, it was pushing against the large Eurasian plate. Between the two plates was an ancient ocean. The rocks formed from sediments piled up on the bed of the ocean were squeezed up into the Himalayas, which form the world's highest mountain range.

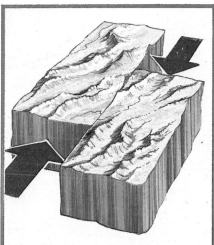

Above: Plates move past each other like two blocks of wood being pushed in opposite directions. But the movement is not smooth. The plate edges are jagged and the plates are usually locked together. But pressure finally breaks the locks. The plates then move suddenly in a violent jerk.

Right: The map shows the plates into which the Earth's surface is divided. The plates are all moving very slowly. The movements cause earthquakes, volcanic eruptions and the creation of mountain ranges.

Ocean Ridges and Trenches

The study of the oceans in recent years has helped to explain how continents move. No rocks in the oceanic crust are much older than 200 million years. This shows that the oceans are young features, unlike the continents, which have rocks dating back 3800 million years. The youngest rocks are in the middle of long, mostly underwater mountain ranges, or ocean ridges. The rocks in the crust become progressively older away from the ridges in both directions. The ocean ridges are earthquake zones. Earthquakes also occur along the deep ocean trenches, near the edges of the oceans.

Moving Plates

Boundaries between large blocks in the Earth's surface, called plates, run through the ocean ridges. Plates consist of the thin crust, including the continents, and part of the upper mantle. Under the ridges, hot fluid material is rising in the mantle and spreading sideways beneath the plates. These movements are pulling the plates apart by 1 to 4 in a year. When the plates move, molten material rises to plug the gaps. It then hardens into new crustal rock.

Along the ocean trenches, however, plates are colliding and one plate is being pushed down beneath another. As it descends, the front edge of the plate is melted. Some plates move apart and some collide with each other. A third kind of movement occurs when plates move alongside each other. They move along long cracks in the surface, called transform faults.

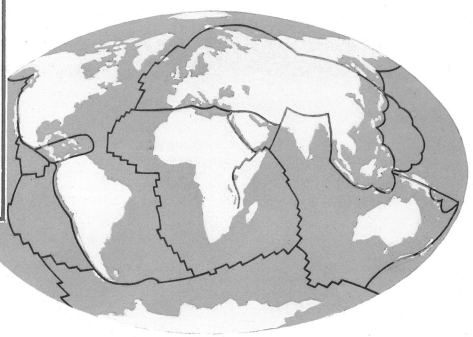

Minerals and Mining

The sand on many beaches is composed largely of a mineral called quartz. Minerals make up all the rocks in the Earth. There are nearly 3000 minerals in the Earth's crust. Some, such as calcite and feldspar, are common. Others, such as diamonds, are rare.

Minerals are made up of elements. Elements are simple substances which cannot be broken down into other substances by chemical methods. Some 92 elements occur naturally in the Earth's crust. But only 22 are ever found in a pure state and samples of them are rare. Elements which occur on their own are called native elements. The other 70 elements all occur in chemical combinations. Minerals which are combinations of elements are called compounds. Metallic minerals contain metals. For example, galena is a metallic mineral containing lead and some silver. Other minerals, such as quartz, are non-metallic.

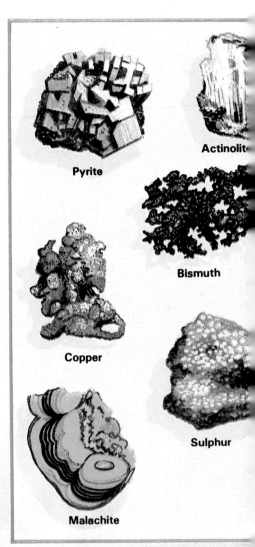

Pyrite

Actinolite

Bismuth

Copper

Sulphur

Malachite

Below: Open-cast mining is used to remove the ores of valuable minerals that are found on or close to the surface.

Right: Minerals occur in many colours. Mineral collecting is a popular hobby. Beautiful crystals are prized by collectors.

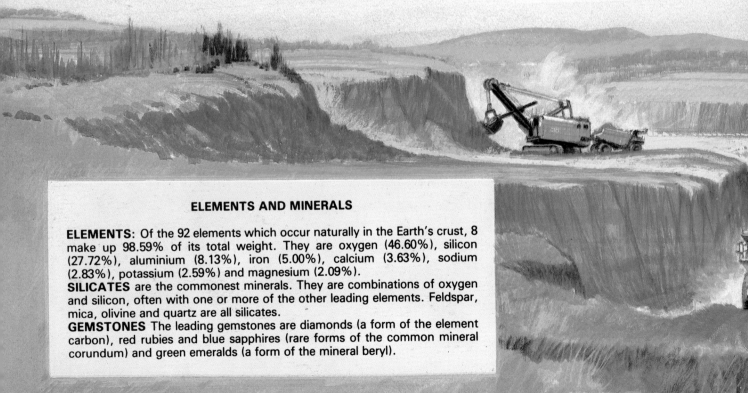

ELEMENTS AND MINERALS

ELEMENTS: Of the 92 elements which occur naturally in the Earth's crust, 8 make up 98.59% of its total weight. They are oxygen (46.60%), silicon (27.72%), aluminium (8.13%), iron (5.00%), calcium (3.63%), sodium (2.83%), potassium (2.59%) and magnesium (2.09%).

SILICATES are the commonest minerals. They are combinations of oxygen and silicon, often with one or more of the other leading elements. Feldspar, mica, olivine and quartz are all silicates.

GEMSTONES The leading gemstones are diamonds (a form of the element carbon), red rubies and blue sapphires (rare forms of the common mineral corundum) and green emeralds (a form of the mineral beryl).

Realgar

Sphalerite

Fluorite

Stibnite

Pyrrhotine

Psilomelane

Galena

Rock crystal

Celestine

MINERAL ORES

NATIVE ELEMEMENTS: Some valuable substances are found in a pure or almost pure state. They are called native elements. They include gold, diamond, silver and sulphur.

MINERAL ORES: Other substances occur in chemical combinations with other elements. Important metals and their ores include:

ALUMINIUM: Bauxite is the chief source of the metal aluminium. It is not a mineral. Instead, it contains several minerals: boehmite, diaspore and gibbsite.

COPPER: The most common copper ore is chalcopyrite. Other copper minerals are azurite, bornite, chalcosine, cuprite and malachite.

IRON: Hematite, magnetite and siderite.

LEAD: Galena and anglesite.

MANGANESE: Psilomelane, pyrolustie.

TIN: Cassiterite.

TUNGSTEN: Wolframite.

ZINC: Sphalerite (or zinc blende).

Rocks of the Earth

Rocks consist of minerals and most rocks contain several minerals. There are three kinds of rocks: igneous rocks, metamorphic rocks and sedimentary rocks.

Igneous Rocks

The term igneous comes from a Latin word meaning 'fire', and all igneous rocks are formed from hot magma. When magma cools slowly underground, coarse-grained igneous rocks are formed. The grains (or mineral crystals) in the rock are visible with the naked eye. The commonest igneous rock formed in this way is granite.

Other igneous rocks form when magma cools quickly in the air or in water. Fast cooling prevents the formation of crystals and so these rocks are fine-grained. To see the minerals in fine-grained rocks, you must study them through a microscope. The commonest fine-grained igneous rock is basalt.

Metamorphic Rocks

When magma rises upwards, it heats the other rocks. Heat changes rocks, just as wet dough is turned into bread in a hot oven. Rocks are also changed by pressure and by chemical action caused by hot steam and liquids.

Rocks changed by heat, pressure or steam are called metamorphic rocks. The hard metamorphic rock slate (used for roofing) was formerly the soft rock shale or mudstone.

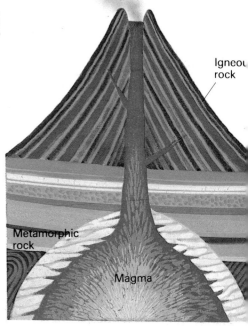

Igneous rock

Metamorphic rock

Magma

Below: The Grand Canyon is one of the most impressive sights in the world. This vast gorge in Arizona, USA, was cut out by the Colorado river, and in places it reaches a depth of about one mile. The successive layers of different colored rocks give its steep walls a striped effect.

Marble is a metamorphic rock formed from limestone. Other metamorphic rocks include gneiss, hornfels and quartzite.

Sedimentary Rocks

Igneous and metamorphic rocks make up 95 per cent of the rocks in the top 10 miles of the Earth's crust. But sedimentary rocks cover 75 per cent of the Earth's land surface.

Many sedimentary rocks consist of worn fragments of other rocks. These fragments are piled up, usually in water, and pressed into layers. The loose grains are later cemented together by minerals deposited from seeping water. Such rocks include sandstone and shale. Some sedimentary rocks are deposited from water. They include flint, rock salt and some kinds of limestone. Other limestones consist largely of the remains of dead sea creatures. Coal is another sedimentary rock. It consists of the remains of ancient plants.

Sedimentary rock

Metamorphic rock

Rock fragments

Igneous rock

Above: The diagram shows the main kinds of rock. Igneous rocks are formed when molten magma is pushed upwards through the Earth's crust and cools and hardens. Some magma reaches the surface and some cools underground. Metamorphic rocks are rocks that have been changed by great heat or by pressure. The third type is called sedimentary rock. Many sedimentary rocks are formed from fragments of sand, mud or the remains of dead sea creatures which pile up in water.

Right: Mountaineers have climbed most of the world's highest peaks, including Mount Everest. Everest is in the Himalayas, on the border between Nepal and China.

Mountains

The four main kinds of mountains are fold mountains, block mountains and volcanic and dome mountains.

Fold Mountains

Folds are bends in layers of rock caused by sideways movements in the Earth's crust. Upfolds are called anticlines and downfolds are called synclines.

Fold mountains rise when two plates in the Earth's crust push against each other. Flat layers of rock between the plates are then buckled upwards into huge loops. For example, the Himalayas are fold mountains caused by a collision between a plate bearing India and another plate bearing the rest of Asia (see pages 16-17). The Alps started to rise when, about 26 million years ago, the African plate pushed a small plate bearing Italy against the underside of Europe.

Block Mountains

When plates move, they crack nearby rocks. Long cracks are called faults. Plate movements cause faults to open up and push the cracked rocks up and down along the faults. Large blocks of land squeezed upwards along faults are called horsts or block mountains.

Volcanic and Dome Mountains

Volcanic mountains are made up of erupted magma. Sometimes magma rises upwards but does not reach the surface. It pushes the overlying rocks up into domes. When the overlying rocks are worn away, the hardened magma is exposed as a dome mountain.

Fold mountains are formed by lateral (sideways) pressure. Flat layers of rock are arched up into folds. Fold mountain ranges include the Himalayas in Asia, the Alps in Europe, the Rockies in North America and the Andes in South America.

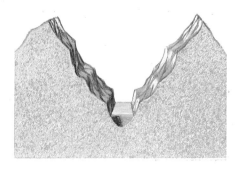

Fast-flowing rivers in mountainous regions wear out deep, V-shaped valleys.

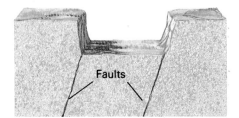

Rift valleys form when blocks of land sink downwards between two sets of faults.

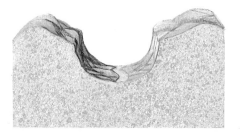

Steep-sided U-shaped valleys are worn out by glaciers (tongues of ice) in mountain regions.

Valleys and Slopes

Even as mountains are pushed upwards, so the forces of erosion start to wear them down. Weathering breaks up rocks. Rivers and glaciers carry worn material away. In doing so, they wear out deep valleys. Rift valleys are not eroded. They are formed when blocks of land slip down between faults.

Steep slopes are the main feature of mountain areas. Rocks on steep slopes are unstable. They may be dislodged by earthquakes to cause landslides, earth flows (movements of fine soil and clay), mud flows (made of dust and sand or volcanic ash mixed with water), and avalanches (falls of ice, snow and rock).

Landslides are movements of soil and rock down a cliff or mountainside. Landslides can do much damage and cause loss of life.

KINDS OF MOUNTAINS

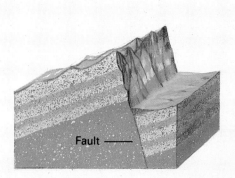

Block mountains are formed when a large block of land is pushed upwards along a fault (crack) or between two faults in the Earth's crust. The Sierra Nevada range in California in the south-western United States is an example of a block mountain.

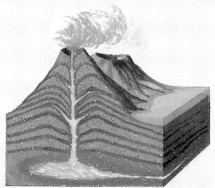

Some volcanic mountains consist of volcanic ash and other fragments of magma which have been exploded into the air. Others are huge piles of hardened lava. Most volcanoes contain layers of ash alternating with layers of lava.

LANDSLIDES AND AVALANCHES

Some of the most destructive landslides and avalanches are caused by earthquakes.

For example, an earthquake in 1840 caused a landslide in the Himalayas. Rocks crashed down a gorge into the Indus River. The rocks dammed the river and a 40-mile long lake formed behind the rocks. When the dam burst, a flood destroyed everything in its path for hundreds of miles downstream.

A landslide in Italy in 1963 sent many rocks crashing into a man-made lake. Water surged over the dam, wiping out the resort of Longarone.

In 1970, an avalanche in Peru killed 18,000 people.

23

Volcanoes

Volcanoes are vents (holes) in the ground where magma reaches the Earth's surface. The magma may appear in flows of molten lava or as fragments, including volcanic ash and sizeable volcanic bombs. Mountains built of magma are also called volcanoes.

There are more than 500 active volcanoes. Active volcanoes have erupted in historic times. Between eruptions, they are dormant (sleeping). Volcanoes that are unlikely to erupt again are extinct.

Where Volcanoes Occur

Most volcanoes lie near the edges of the moving plates in the Earth's crust (see pages 16-17). Some are on the ocean ridges. Others are near places where one plate is descending beneath another. The descending plate is melted to produce magma. A few volcanoes, like those in Hawaii, lie far from plate edges. They are probably above hot spots in the Earth's mantle.

Right: This diagram of a volcano shows that magma rises from an underground chamber (1) to the crater (2) during eruptions. Ash is sometimes exploded into the air while lava (3) flows from the crater. The ash and lava pile up to form a volcanic mountain. Sheets of magma are forced into nearby rocks. Some called dykes (4) cut across existing layers, while sills (5) run between existing layers. Some magma may be forced through secondary vents (6) in the side of the mountain. Runny lava may rise through long faults (7) and spread out over the land. Extinct volcanoes (8) have not erupted in historic times. Magma heats water in the rocks. Some water appears in hot springs and geysers (9), which are high jets of hot water and steam.

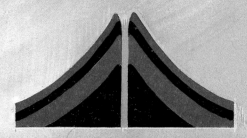
Volcanoes formed from ash and cinder are steep-sided. Cones like these often build up inside craters between major eruptions.

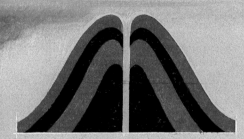
Thick, pasty lava flows only a short distance before it hardens. It also forms volcanic mountains with steep slopes.

Runny lava flows great distances. As a result, it forms flattened volcanoes, like upturned saucers, as in Hawaii.

Kinds of Volcanoes

Some volcanoes erupt in huge explosions. These volcanoes contain pasty magma. Lots of gases and steam are trapped in the magma. The vent of the volcano is usually blocked by a hard plug of magma. Below, the magma is pushing upwards until the pressure becomes so great that the plug is removed. Hot gases and steam then surge from the vent, often followed by a dark cloud of hot ash which races down the mountainside. Huge columns of ash are hurled into the air.

Quiet volcanoes, by contrast, usually contain runny magma, from which gases and steam can easily escape. They do not erupt in great explosions. Instead, they emit long streams of fluid lava. However, most volcanoes are intermediate in type. They sometimes erupt explosively and sometimes quietly.

Predicting Eruptions

Scientists keep watch on many active volcanoes. They look out for small earthquakes, swellings in the sides of the mountains and increases in temperatures and pressure. When they think an eruption is likely, they warn people and ask them to leave the area.

GREAT VOLCANIC ERUPTIONS

GREATEST VOLCANIC EXPLOSION: A volcano on the Greek island of Thera (Santorini) exploded in about 1470 BC with the power of about 130 times the greatest H-bomb detonation.
GREATEST MODERN EXPLOSION: People 3000 miles away heard the volcanic explosion on the Indonesian island of Krakatoa in 1883. But this explosion was probably only about one-fifth as powerful as that at Thera.
GREATEST ERUPTION: Tambora, a volcano on the Indonesian island of Sumbawa, erupted in 1815. It was the greatest in terms of the amount of rock removed. The total amount of rock exploded away was probably two and a half to three times as much as at Thera.

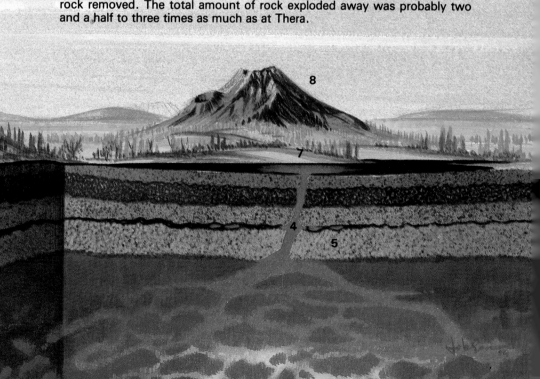

Earthquakes

The Trembling Earth

Earthquakes can occur anywhere. They may be caused by landslides or by volcanic eruptions. But most are caused by movements along faults in rocks which shake the land. Most do little or no damage. But a few earthquakes cause great destruction.

The place inside the Earth where an earthquake occurs is called the focus. The most destructive earthquakes have a focus that is within about 40 miles of the surface. Earth movements at much deeper levels have less effect at the surface. The point on the surface above the focus is called the epicenter. The epicenters of many earthquakes are in the oceans. The tremors may set off fast moving waves called tsunamis. Tsunamis can cause great damage far away from the epicenter.

Below: The map shows that most earthquakes occur in clearly defined zones. Earthquakes can occur anywhere, but most of them, including the most intense, are concentrated around the edges of the moving plates into which the Earth's crust is divided.

Bottom: During severe earthquakes, like the one that hit Anchorage and other towns in Alaska in 1964, large cracks may open up in the shaking ground. Buildings collapse and landslides often cause great damage. Other hazards include fires, which often do even more damage than the earthquake, and tsunamis (high waves) that strike coastal areas, sweeping ships inland.

Red dots show major earthquake regions

Where Earthquakes Occur

The chief earthquake zones follow the edges of the plates in the Earth's crust, namely the ocean ridges, zones where one plate is descending beneath another, and transform faults. Earthquakes occur when plates move in sudden jerks. The San Andreas (transform) fault runs through California, in the south-western USA. A movement along this fault in 1906 shook the city of San Francisco. Fires destroyed much property. Since 1906, scientists have found ways of building houses that will not collapse during 'quakes.

Earthquake Prediction

Scientists want to find ways of predicting earthquakes. They have discovered that rocks may be deformed as pressure builds up before a 'quake. Other changes in rocks and even unusual behaviour by animals, which seem to sense danger, are also being studied. But earthquake forecasting is still a young science.

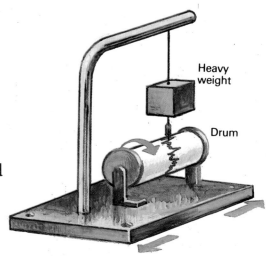

Heavy weight

Drum

Above: Seismographs are sensitive instruments used to record earthquakes. When an earthquake occurs, the heavy weight suspended from the frame stays almost still while the support shakes. The vibrations are recorded on a piece of paper wrapped around a slowly revolving drum.

Shaping the Land

Right: Limestone caves are worn out by rainwater. Limestone consists mostly of calcium carbonate. This substance reacts chemically with rainwater, which eats away the rock along the horizontal and vertical cracks in the rock. Water seeping through the caves is highly charged with calcium carbonate.

Water dripping from the roof of a cave is often agitated and evaporated by air currents. Thin films of the mineral calcite are then deposited from the water. Layer upon layer of such deposits build downwards to form the icicle-like stalactites. Water splashing onto the floor of a cave also deposits calcite. These build upwards into stalagmites.

Although it is difficult to see, the land in your home area is slowly changing. American scientists have worked out that about one foot of land is removed from the eastern USA every 9000 years. This may not seem much. But if you remember that we measure Earth history in millions of years, you will realize that mountains can be worn down to plains. The main forces that shape the land are weathering, winds, rivers, ice and, along coasts, sea waves.

Weathering occurs in several ways. For example, rain is important, because some minerals, such as rock salt, dissolve in water. Some rocks, such as limestones, do not dissolve in pure water. But limestone dissolves in water which contains carbon dioxide dissolved from the air or soil. The dissolved gas changes the water into a weak acid. This acid wears out limestone caves.

Rainwater also affects the hard rock granite. This is because water combines with some kinds of feldspar and turns them into clay. The quartz and mica in granite are not affected. Grains of these minerals are washed away by rain and rivers. The quartz grains often form sandy beaches along coasts.

Above: Plants contribute to the break-up of rocks. Here, a seedling has taken root in a crack in a boulder. As the tree grows, the roots exert great pressure, pushing the boulder apart.

28

Weathering in Mountains and Deserts

In mountain areas, water seeps into cracks in rocks during the day. At night, temperatures often fall below zero and the water freezes. Ice occupies nine per cent more space than the same amount of water and so, when water freezes, it expands and the ice pushes against the sides of cracks. When this happens night after night, the cracks are widened and the rocks are finally split apart. This is called frost action. The shattered rocks tumble downhill. They often pile up in heaps called talus or scree.

In deserts, rocks are heated by the Sun by day. In the evening, temperatures fall quickly, often to below freezing point. The fast cooling of the rocks cracks the surfaces, making sounds like pistol shots. Layers of rock then peel away.

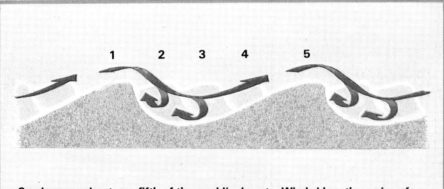

Sand covers about one-fifth of the world's deserts. Winds blow the grains of sand around, piling them up into hills called dunes. Dunes move in the direction of the prevailing (usual) wind. Grains of sand are blown up the gentle windward slopes and then topple down the steep slip faces. In this way, the dune slowly advances from position 1 to 2, 3, 4, 5 and so on.

Plants and Animals

As shown in the picture on the facing page, the roots of trees and shrubs can split rocks apart and so they also contribute to weathering. But plants also protect the land, especially when grass roots bind loose soil particles together.

Worms, which eat vast amounts of soil, and burrowing animals, such as rodents and termites, also play their part, because churned up soil is easily removed by rain and wind.

Right: Many desert features were carved by water at times in the past when the desert had a moist climate. Today, wind-blown sand eats away rocks along lines of weakness and polishes rocks, such as this natural arch.

DESERT LANDSCAPES

There are three main kinds of desert landscapes: sandy deserts called *erg*; stony deserts called *reg*; and bare rocky deserts called *hammada*.

Deserts have little rain, but the main land features in most deserts were carved out by running water at a time when the climate was very different from that of today. Even now, a rare thunderstorm can drown areas which have been dry for years. *Wadis* (dry valleys) fill up with rushing torrents that sweep huge amounts of sand and rock away.

But wind-blown sand is the main natural form of erosion in deserts today. It can strip the paint off cars and undercut telegraph poles and boulders. It is responsible for mushroom-shaped boulders with a large top resting on a narrow stem. Wind-blown sand also grinds out deep hollows in rocky surfaces.

In sandy deserts, the wind blows the sand into dunes. *Barchans* are crescent-shaped dunes, while *seif dunes* are long sand ridges.

The Work of Rivers

Running water is a major force in shaping the land. In itself, water has little power to erode (wear away) rock. But rivers push loose boulders, stones and sand along their courses. As they do so, the loose material scrapes the river bed and loosens other rocks. In this way, rivers can wear out deep valleys. River water also dissolves some rocks. Of all the material carried by rivers, about 30 per cent is dissolved rock and 70 per cent is solid material. Most rivers can be divided into three distinctive stages. They are called youth, maturity and old age.

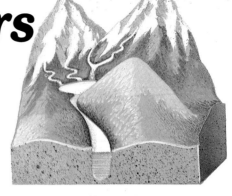

Above: Youthful rivers rise in glaciers, lakes or springs. They flow swiftly downhill and wear out deep V-shaped valleys. Erosion occurs when the river is in flood.

Youthful Rivers

Rivers originate in several ways. Some flow from melting glaciers. Some drain out of lakes. Others start in springs where water bubbles to the surface.

In mountain areas, youthful rivers flow rapidly straight down steep slopes. After rains or when snow melts in spring, they become raging torrents. They then wear away their beds and carve out deep, V-shaped valleys.

Right: The diagram shows features of a river in old age. On straight stretches, the channel is symmetrical (1). On bends, the outer bend is undercut, but sediment is dumped on the inner bend (2). In old age, when a river floods, particles are dumped on the river banks to form mounds called levees (3). Other features are oxbow lakes (abandoned meanders) and deltas where the river divides into channels.

Above: In middle age, rivers develop meanders (bends) and so lateral (sideways) erosion becomes more important than downward erosion. As a result, the valleys become broader and broader.

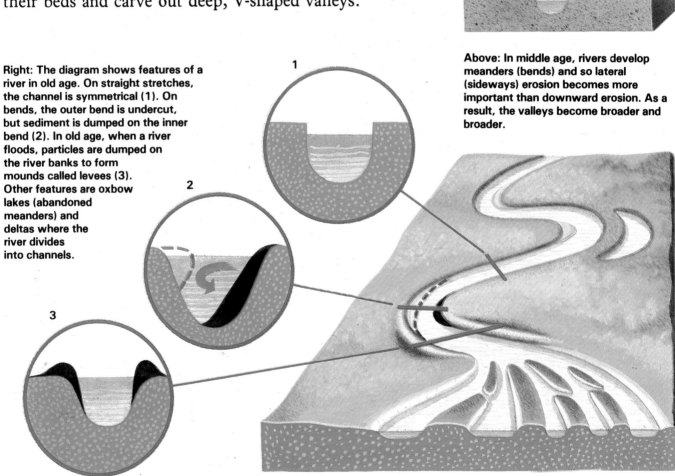

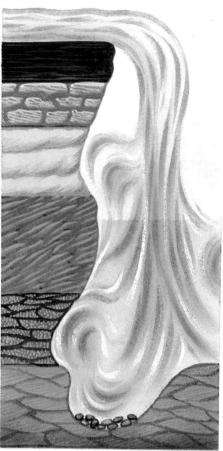

Left: In dry areas, fast-flowing rivers carve out deep gorges, as in the Big Bend part of the Rio Grande's course in Texas, USA.

Below: A section through a waterfall showing how the water undercuts the base of the rock face.

Mature Rivers

When rivers emerge from mountains, they slow down as they flow over less steep slopes. They develop large, sweeping bends, called meanders. Mature rivers do not deepen their valleys like youthful rivers. But the strong currents constantly widen the valleys.

Old Age Rivers

In old age, rivers flow slowly across nearly flat plains. There is little erosion, although the rivers carry huge amounts of fine sediment. When the rivers overflow, the sediment is spread over the land. Large particles are dropped on the river banks, where they pile up to form mounds called levees. Fine particles are swept long distances from the river.

In old age, rivers sometimes change course. They cut through the necks of bends and so straighten their courses. The bends then become 'abandoned meanders', or oxbow lakes, which later dry up. Some rivers dump much of their load of sediment at their mouths in areas called deltas. But in places where tidal currents are strong, the sediment is swept out to sea.

WATERFALLS

Many waterfalls, including Niagara Falls in North America, occur where rivers flow over hard rocks that resist erosion. The diagram, above, shows a waterfall of this kind. The softer rocks below are undercut so that, occasionally, parts of the overlying rock break off and crash down. Such falls gradually retreat upstream. On average, Niagara Falls is retreating by about 3 feet a year.

Other falls occur along steep escarpments that separate highlands from lowlands. Others occur in glaciated regions, where rivers plunge into deep U-shaped valleys.

The world's highest waterfall is Angel Falls, Venezuela. It is 3245 feet high.

The Water's Edge

The sea is never still and, on stormy days, high waves crash against the shore. The waves trap air in cracks in rocks and compress it. When the pressure is released, the air expands again with considerable force, which may enlarge the cracks and shatter the rock. Waves also pick up loose rocks and throw them at the shore. This bombardment undercuts cliffs and breaks up loose rocks into smaller and smaller pieces.

Wave erosion removes soft rocks, such as the loose material deposited by ice sheets, far faster than hard rocks, such as granite or limestone. Rapidly eroded areas form bays, while hard rocks may remain as headlands. But, as shown in the picture on this page, caves and arches are worn into headlands. When the arches collapse, rocky islands, called stacks, are left behind. They, too, are eventually removed.

Longshore Drift

Waves and currents drag some of the eroded material out to sea. But in places they carry material along the coast, often in a zig-zag direction, as shown in the diagram on the next page. This is called longshore drift. It is responsible for various land features which are built up by wave action.

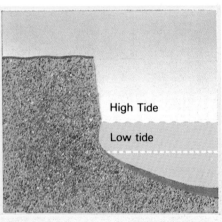

High Tide

Low tide

Below: Waves wear away soft rocks to form bays, while harder rocks form headlands. Wave action wears caves into the sides of headlands. Blow-holes are holes in the roofs of caves through which spray is thrown. When two caves meet, an arch is formed. When the arch collapses, the end of the headland becomes a stack.

Blow-hole

Stacks

Cave

Arch

VANISHING COASTLINES

Cliffs on Martha's Vineyard, an island in Massachusetts, in the USA, are being cut back by about 5 feet a year. A lighthouse has had to be rebuilt three times.

When the Romans conquered Britain in AD 43, the Holderness coast of Humberside, in northern England, stretched 2 miles farther out to sea than it does today. Many towns shown on old maps have vanished beneath the waves.

The coasts of Holderness and Martha's Vineyard have something in common. They are both composed of loose rocks deposited by ice sheets. These soft rocks are more easily removed by waves than harder rocks.

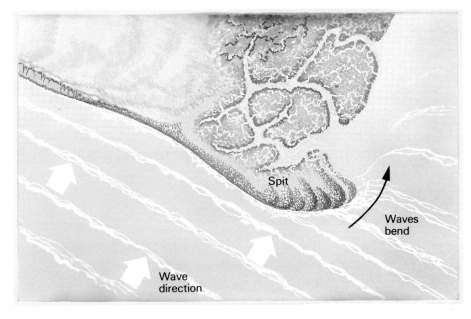

Spit

Waves bend

Wave direction

Opposite and above: Wave erosion occurs between high and low tide level. In this zone, storm waves hurl loose rocks at the shore and wear out hollows in the cliffs.

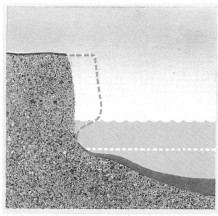

Above: The hollowing out of the bottom of cliffs continues until part of the cliff collapses. The shattered rocks on the shore are broken up and carried away.

Spits are low ridges of sand and pebbles built up by waves and currents. They usually occur at places where the coast changes direction. Spits often develop curved hooks at the ends.

Bars and Spits

Material carried along a coast is often dumped to form low ridges in the sea. Some, called bars, are not connected to the land. But spits extend outwards from the coast. Some extend across bays. They may seal off large areas of water to form lakes called lagoons.

A spit that links an island to the mainland is called a tombolo. For example, Chesil Beach in Dorset, England, is a long tombolo.

Other spits build up from two facing headlands, meeting up at an angle. Spits of this kind are found on the coasts of the eastern USA.

Longshore drift removes sandy beaches at seaside resorts. In order to keep the beaches, sea walls called groynes are built into the sea at right angles to the shore.

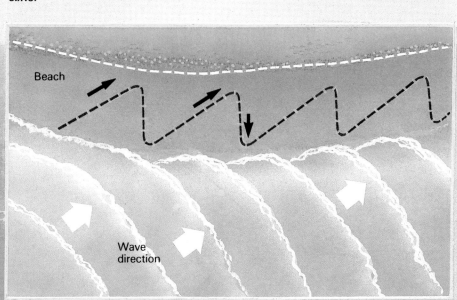

Beach

Wave direction

Left: Waves usually surge up the shore at an angle. But, because of gravity, the backwash returns at right angles to the shore. This zig-zag motion is responsible for the movement of sand and pebbles along a coast. This movement is called longshore drift.

Rivers of Ice

Ice covers about one tenth of the world's land areas. Most of the ice is in two great ice sheets covering Antarctica and Greenland. There are also smaller ice caps and many valley glaciers (rivers of ice) in mountain regions. But around 12,000 years ago, during the Ice Age, ice covered three times the present area.

Moving Ice

Ice sheets, ice caps and valley glaciers form in places where all the winter snow does not melt in summer. Instead, it piles up until it is slowly compacted into ice.

In mountain regions, glacier ice forms in basins, called cirques. It spills out of these basins and flows downhill, often joining up with other glaciers. The moving ice carries loose weathered rocks on its surface. The surface is pitted with cracks called crevasses. Many rocks fall into the crevasses and are frozen within the ice. Some glaciers end at a 'snout', where the ice melts and dumps the debris, or moraine. Others reach the sea and icebergs break off and float away.

Above: The map of the world shows the parts of the northern hemisphere that were covered by ice during the recent Ice Age. Mountain regions in central and southern Eurasia also had far more ice than they have today.

Below: Animals with plenty of hair, such as the woolly mammoth, were well equipped to survive the cold during the Ice Age. But the woolly mammoth was hunted to extinction by prehistoric hunters.

Glaciation

Moving bodies of ice have rocks frozen into their sides and bottoms. These rocks scrape against the land and wear away the underlying rocks. They deepen the basins (cirques) where the ice is formed. They carve out U-shaped valleys and other features shown in the diagrams on this page. Many of the world's lakes occupy ice-worn basins or basins dammed by moraine.

At the snouts of glaciers, some moraine piles up in long ridges. Other material, ranging from sizeable boulders to fine 'rock flour', is carried away from the ice by streams formed from meltwater.

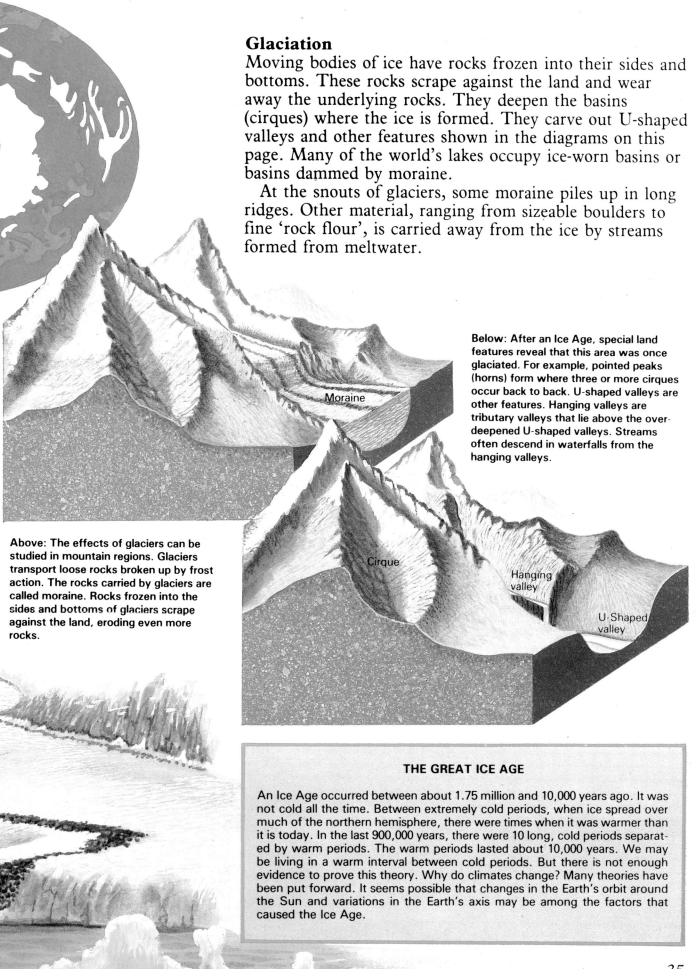

Below: After an Ice Age, special land features reveal that this area was once glaciated. For example, pointed peaks (horns) form where three or more cirques occur back to back. U-shaped valleys are other features. Hanging valleys are tributary valleys that lie above the over-deepened U-shaped valleys. Streams often descend in waterfalls from the hanging valleys.

Moraine

Above: The effects of glaciers can be studied in mountain regions. Glaciers transport loose rocks broken up by frost action. The rocks carried by glaciers are called moraine. Rocks frozen into the sides and bottoms of glaciers scrape against the land, eroding even more rocks.

Cirque

Hanging valley

U-Shaped valley

THE GREAT ICE AGE

An Ice Age occurred between about 1.75 million and 10,000 years ago. It was not cold all the time. Between extremely cold periods, when ice spread over much of the northern hemisphere, there were times when it was warmer than it is today. In the last 900,000 years, there were 10 long, cold periods separated by warm periods. The warm periods lasted about 10,000 years. We may be living in a warm interval between cold periods. But there is not enough evidence to prove this theory. Why do climates change? Many theories have been put forward. It seems possible that changes in the Earth's orbit around the Sun and variations in the Earth's axis may be among the factors that caused the Ice Age.

Mapping the Land

Maps show the world or parts of it on flat surfaces. Accurate maps are drawn to scale. At a scale of 1:50,000, 1 inch on the map equals 50,000 inches on the ground.

Surveying the Land

The first job of land surveyors (people who measure the land) is to fix as accurately as possible the positions of a network of points, by measuring the angles and distances between them. Surveyors use telescopic instruments, theodolites, to measure angles. Measuring distances was once a slow process, using metal tapes. But surveyors can now use electronic instruments. When the positions of the points are known, their heights are measured. These fixed points, which are often marked on the ground by concrete pillars, form the skeleton of a map.

MAP SYMBOLS

CONTOURS are lines joining places with the same height. They are usually brown lines, but underwater contours are blue.

CULTURAL FEATURES are man-made things, such as towns, churches, historical sites, including battlefields (crossed swords), lighthouses, roads and railroads. They usually appear in red or black.

HACHURES are fine lines that show land forms three-dimensionally.

LAYER TINTING is the use of colors and shades of colors to show the various levels of the land.

SPOT HEIGHTS are black dots or solid black triangles. A figure in metres or feet alongside the point shows the exact height.

VEGETATION FEATURES, such as forests and swamps, are usually depicted as green symbols.

WATER FEATURES, such as rivers, lakes and coasts, are shown in blue.

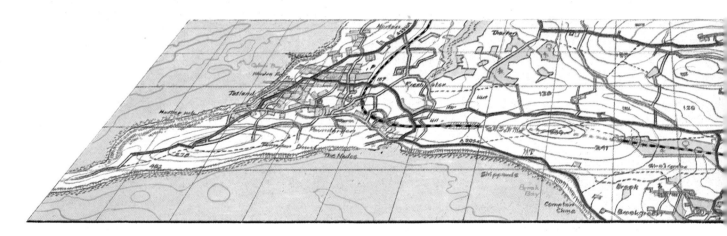

Detailed Mapping

When the network of points is fixed, surveyors must measure all the details of the land between them. This work was once done on the ground. But, today, mapping from air photographs has largely replaced ground mapping.

Aircraft take long strips of photographs of the land. Each photograph overlaps the next by 60 per cent. The fixed ground points are identified on the photographs. Because the distances between them are known, other distances can be measured on the photographs.

Heights can also be measured. This is because overlapping photographs viewed through a stereoscope appear as a three-dimensional model of the land.

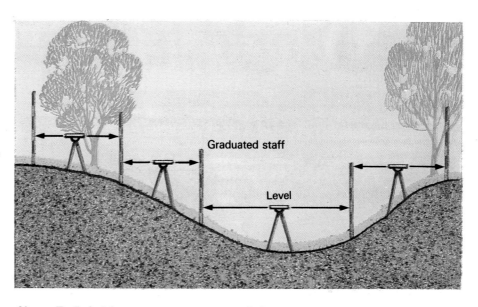

Above: To fix heights, surveyors use a telescopic instrument called a level, which is mounted on a tripod, and a graduated staff. The difference between the height of the level and a reading on the staff is the height difference between the two points.

Below: Topographic maps, or general reference maps, show the main features of the land over fairly small areas. They are drawn to scale so that any distance on the map represents a distance on the ground. In order to include as many details as possible, map-makers use symbols like those shown below. You will find a legend (key), containing all the symbols used on a map in the margins of most topographic maps.

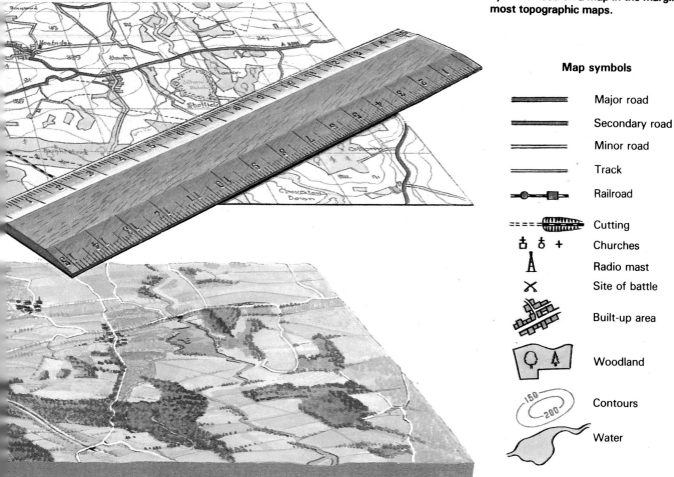

Map symbols

Major road
Secondary road
Minor road
Track
Railroad
Cutting
Churches
Radio mast
Site of battle
Built-up area
Woodland
Contours
Water

The World is Round

Geographers are interested in features on the Earth's surface and how the features are related to one another. The best way to present the information which geographers need is a map. The facts on a map would often fill a book.

Types of Maps

Apart from topographic, or general reference, maps, there are many special kinds of maps. For example, weather maps show the weather conditions over a large area, and population maps show where people are most concentrated. Special maps are now often produced by computers. They can be a great help to planners.

Some maps are large-scale, covering small areas. Maps with extremely large scales are called *plans*. But small-scale maps cover large areas. Such maps appear in atlases. Small-scale maps create problems for map-makers.

Curved Surfaces, Flat Maps

A major problem faced by map-makers is that the Earth is nearly a sphere. Its surface is curved, not flat. To understand the problem, think of another sphere, an orange.

If you peel an orange, keeping the peel in one piece, you are left with a hollow sphere. It is impossible to turn this sphere into a flat surface without breaking it and crushing the pieces. To deal with this problem, map-makers have devised various solutions — map projections.

Map Projections

Map projections are ways of *projecting* details on a curved surface onto a flat surface.

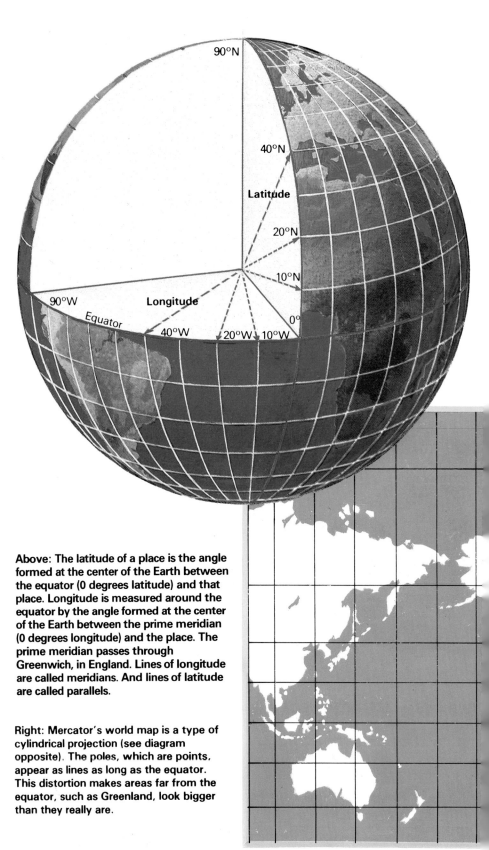

Above: The latitude of a place is the angle formed at the center of the Earth between the equator (0 degrees latitude) and that place. Longitude is measured around the equator by the angle formed at the center of the Earth between the prime meridian (0 degrees longitude) and the place. The prime meridian passes through Greenwich, in England. Lines of longitude are called meridians. And lines of latitude are called parallels.

Right: Mercator's world map is a type of cylindrical projection (see diagram opposite). The poles, which are points, appear as lines as long as the equator. This distortion makes areas far from the equator, such as Greenland, look bigger than they really are.

Some projections are devised as though the Earth is a glass sphere with all the details and lines of latitude and longitude engraved on it. If you place a light at the centre of the globe, the engraved lines are projected as shadows onto flat surfaces. A cylindrical projection of this type is shown below. But most projections are worked out by mathematics.

No one map can show shapes, areas, distances and directions correctly at the same time. Only a globe can do that. Some map projections preserve some features and some preserve others. Equal area maps, for instance, ensure that all countries are the right *size*. Conformal maps make sure that the *shape* of the countries is correct. The type of projection depends on the purpose of the map.

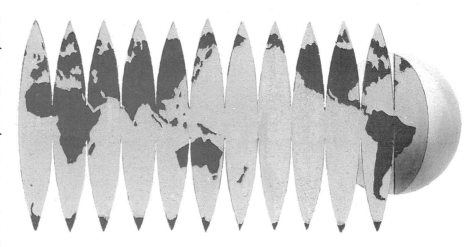

Above: The problem of showing a curved surface on a flat piece of paper is revealed when globes are made. The world map is first printed on a series of thin, lens-shaped pieces of paper, called gores. The gores are fitted together on the globe and pasted down. Some map projections are drawn in separate sections, resembling gores. Such projections are said to be interrupted. Maps based on interrupted projections are of little use, however, because they split up land masses.

Below: Cylindrical map projections are developed as though a light was placed at the centre of an engraved glass globe. Around the globe is a cylinder of paper, touching the globe along the equator. The light casts shadows of the engraved meridians and parallels, together with the shapes of the continents, onto the paper. This creates a map. But you can see that the distances between lines of latitude increase towards the poles. On a true map, these distances should be the same.

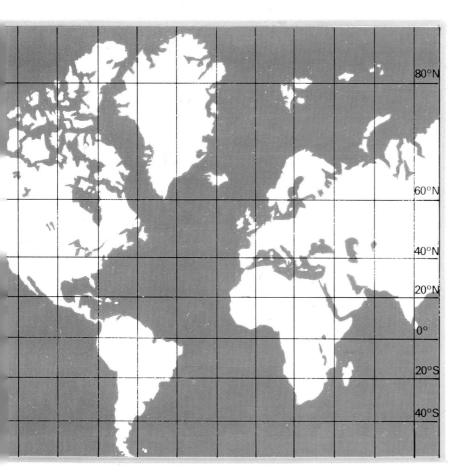

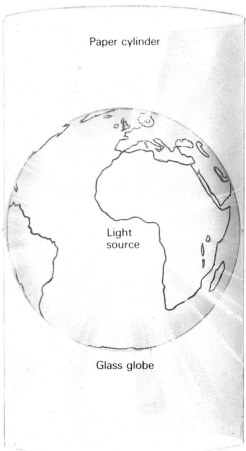

Paper cylinder

Light source

Glass globe

An Ocean of Air

We live in an ocean of air which envelopes the Earth. This thin layer, called the atmosphere, contains the oxygen which people and animals need to breathe and the carbon dioxide that plants need in order to grow. The air also contains moisture in the form of invisible water vapor or visible clouds and fog.

A Protective Shield

The atmosphere is also a shield. It is divided into several layers, which are more and more rarefied as one travels upwards. In the stratosphere, the second layer of the atmosphere, the air is much thinner than at the surface. But this layer contains a gas called ozone. This gas filters out harmful ultraviolet radiation emitted from the Sun. If this radiation were to reach the ground, life on land would be impossible. The atmosphere also stops the Earth from becoming too cold. When the Sun's rays warm the surface, heat is radiated back into the air. If there were no atmosphere, this heat would escape into space. We would then have hot days and bitterly cold nights. But the atmosphere absorbs some of the radiated heat, acting much like a greenhouse.

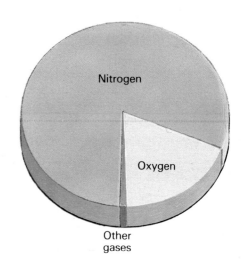

Above: Nitrogen and oxygen make up 99.04% of the air, while argon makes up 0.93%. The other gases, including carbon dioxide, make up 0.03%.

Opposite: The atmosphere contains several layers. Most of the mass of the atmosphere is in the troposphere, the lowest layer. Temperatures fall when one goes upwards. But the temperature stops falling about 11 miles (18 km) up above the equator and 5 miles (8 km) up above the poles. This is the tropopause, or the top of the troposphere. Here the temperature is about −57°C. Above is the stratosphere, which extends up to 30 miles (50 km) above the surface. Temperatures rise again, reaching 0°C at the top of the stratosphere. In the mesosphere, between 30 and 50 miles up, temperatures fall again. In the ionosphere, temperatures rise steadily. At about 300 miles the exosphere merges into space.

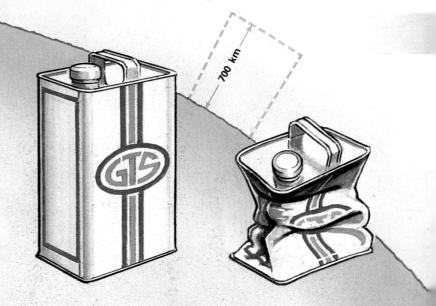

The atmosphere is a thin layer of air that surrounds the Earth. Although we cannot see it, the air has weight. In fact, at this moment, a column of air weighing about a ton is pressing on your shoulders. But you cannot feel this pressure, because there is an equal pressure inside your body. The air inside a metal can weighs about the same as a tablet you might take for a headache. If you pump this air out of the can, creating a vacuum inside it, then the air pressure is powerful enough to crumple the can.

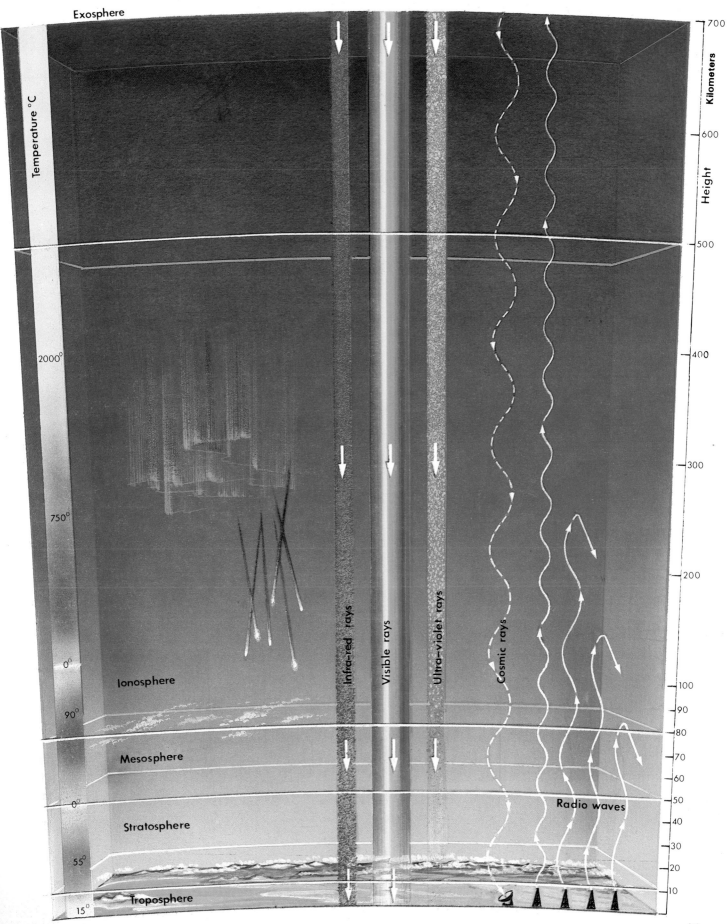

Exosphere

Temperature °C

2000°

750°

0°

90°

0°

55°

15°

Ionosphere

Mesosphere

Stratosphere

Troposphere

Infra-red rays

Visible rays

Ultra-violet rays

Cosmic rays

Radio waves

Kilometers

Height

700

600

500

400

300

200

100

90

80

70

60

50

40

30

20

10

Cloud, Wind and Rain

Air is always moving because of the Sun's heat. At the equator, hot air rises. This creates a zone of low air pressure at the surface, called the *doldrums*. The rising air eventually cools and spreads out north and south. It finally sinks back to the Earth at around latitude 30° North and 30° South. These are the *horse latitudes*. Regions where air is sinking are high air pressure zones. From the horse latitudes, trade winds blow towards the equator and westerly winds blow towards the poles. From the poles — also high air pressure regions — come the polar easterlies. The trade winds, westerlies and polar easterlies are the prevailing (chief) winds of their various regions.

The Sun evaporates water from the oceans. Warm air can hold more water vapor than cold air. But when warm air rises and cools, it finally reaches *dew point*, when the air contains all the vapor it can at that temperature. More cooling makes water vapor *condense* (liquefy) into water droplets or ice crystals, which form clouds. In clouds, water droplets collide to become raindrops. The ice crystals also grow in size. They fall as snow or, in warm air, as raindrops.

Cirrus (a high cloud) is wispy and made of ice crystals.

Cirrocumulus (a high cloud) is thin with ripples or rounded masses.

Cirrostratus (a high cloud) may cause halos around the Sun or Moon.

Altocumulus (a medium cloud) consists of rounded masses.

Altostratus (a medium cloud) is a grayish sheet cloud.

Cumulus (a low cloud) is a white heap cloud.

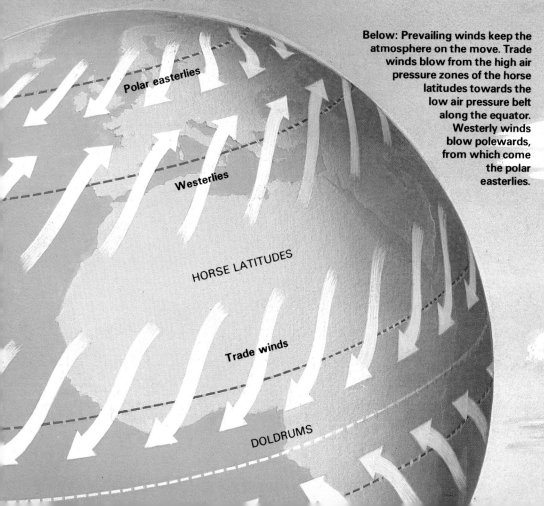

Below: Prevailing winds keep the atmosphere on the move. Trade winds blow from the high air pressure zones of the horse latitudes towards the low air pressure belt along the equator. Westerly winds blow polewards, from which come the polar easterlies.

Polar easterlies

Westerlies

HORSE LATITUDES

Trade winds

DOLDRUMS

(1) Orographic rain occurs when winds blow over mountains. The rising air cools, clouds form and rain falls on the windward slopes. Beyond the mountain tops, the air descends and gets warmer, drying the land. This is a rain shadow region.

(2) Convectional rain occurs when the Sun heats the Earth's surface which, in turn, heats the air near the ground. The warm air rises in fast currents. Eventually, the rising air cools, clouds form and rain starts to fall.

(3) Cyclonic rain occurs in depressions (or cyclones) when warm air rises above blocks of cold air.

Cumulonimbus (thundercloud) may extend from 1000 to 40,000 feet.

Stratus (a low cloud) is a gray layer cloud.

Storm and Tempest

About 45,000 thunderstorms occur every day around the world. They form when warm air rises rapidly, creating towering cumulonimbus clouds.

Some thunderstorms occur along cold fronts in the depressions that bring stormy weather to temperate regions. Others occur in tropical areas. Here, the Sun heats the surface in the morning and strong currents of air sweep water vapor upwards. Huge cumulonimbus clouds with anvil-shaped tops form and raindrops start to fall in the late afternoon. Following a storm, the sky clears in the early evening.

Less common, but more dangerous storms are hurricanes, which occur north and south of the doldrums. Hurricanes have caused millions of dollars' worth of damage in the south-eastern USA. The USA is also hit by whirlwinds, or tornadoes. A tornado in 1925 killed 689 people in the south-central USA in three hours.

HURRICANES

Because of their size and high wind speeds, which reach 180 mph, hurricanes are the most destructive storms. They form over the oceans a little way north and south of the equator. They are also called tropical cyclones, typhoons or willy-willies.

When these storms approach land, they cause floods. About 11 strike the coasts of North America every year. They are tracked by the Hurricane Warning Service at Miami, Florida. The meteorologists use satellite photographs and reports from ships and aircraft in order to discover in which direction and at what speed the hurricanes are moving.

Below: The diagram shows a depression moving from left to right. High cirrus clouds appear ahead of the warm front. Medium and low clouds follow and rain falls. Thunderstorms are features of the cold front.

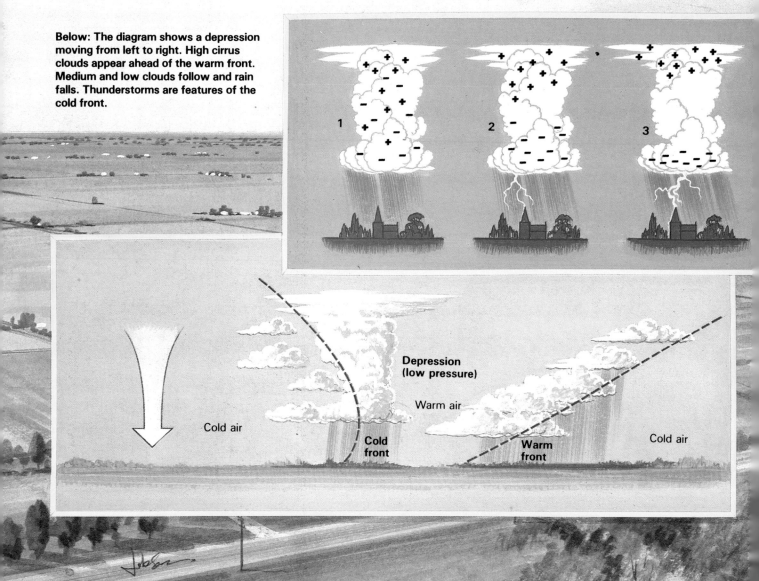

Depression (low pressure)

Warm air

Cold air

Cold front

Warm front

Cold air

Right: Tornadoes are small but destructive storms. About 500 to 600 hit the mid-western USA every year. They form when a funnel-like column of air sinks down from a thundercloud. Warm air rises and swirls around this column. At ground level, tornadoes are only about 400 yards. But wind speeds may reach 400 mph and people may be lifted into the air.

Left: Lightning occurs in cumulonimbus clouds, because positive electrical charges build up in the tops of clouds and negative charges at the bottom (1). When the charges have separated, the electricity is often discharged in a probe stroke (2) and a bright return flash (3). Lightning also leaps from the base of clouds to the positively charged ground. Thunder is caused by the intense heat along the channel followed by the lightning. We see lightning before we hear thunder, because light reaches us faster than sound.

Tomorrow's Weather

Ships' navigators and airline pilots depend for their safety on weather forecasts, while farmers need them so that they can protect their crops. Also millions of ordinary people plan tomorrow's activities only after they have checked the local weather forecast.

Weather Stations

Meteorologists at weather stations on land and at sea collect information about the weather every few hours. They use thermometers to measure temperatures, barometers to measure the air pressure and hygrometers to measure the humidity (moistness) of the air. They also record wind speeds and directions, rainfall amounts, hours of sunshine, cloud types and the visibility. Radiosondes send back readings of the temperature, pressure and humidity at various levels in the upper air (see the diagram on the facing page).

Weather satellites provide pictures of the cloud patterns on Earth, while radar networks show areas where rain or snow is falling. All the information obtained at weather stations is sent, in code, to weather forecasting centers.

Weather symbols		Wind speed (in knots)	
═	Mist	◎	Calm
≡	Fog	⊸○	1-2
❟	Drizzle	⊸○	13-17
●	Rain	◄○	48-52
◉	Sleet	Cloud cover (in eighths)	
✹	Snow	○	None
▽	Shower	◐	1 or less
△	Hail	◑	4
⌐	Thunder	⊗	Total
∞	Haze	Warm front	
⌇	Smoke haze	Cold front	
⌄	Squall	Stationary front	
		Occluded front	

Preparing Weather Forecasts

At weather centers, the information from many weather stations is fed into a computer. The computer produces weather charts which show weather conditions at various levels of the atmosphere. These charts cover extremely large areas. Meteorologists study these charts and find out how the weather has been changing in recent hours. This gives them a good idea of how the weather will change over the next 12 to 24 hours. They summarize their ideas on *prognostic* (forecast) charts. Written forecasts for particular areas are then prepared from the charts. These are sent to newspapers and radio and television stations.

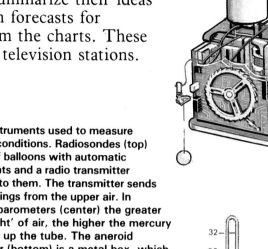

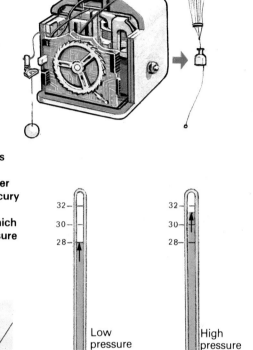

Opposite: Weather satellites circle the Earth taking regular photographs of the changing cloud patterns and collecting information about the upper air.

Below: Weather charts, like topographic maps, use many symbols which indicate weather conditions at various places. The numbered lines, resembling contours, are isobars. Isobars join places with the same air pressure. The fronts are zones of unsettled weather.

Right: Instruments used to measure weather conditions. Radiosondes (top) consist of balloons with automatic instruments and a radio transmitter attached to them. The transmitter sends back readings from the upper air. In mercury barometers (center) the greater the 'weight' of air, the higher the mercury is pushed up the tube. The aneroid barometer (bottom) is a metal box, which expands and contracts as the air pressure changes. This makes a pointer move.

Low pressure

High pressure

Mercury

Mercury

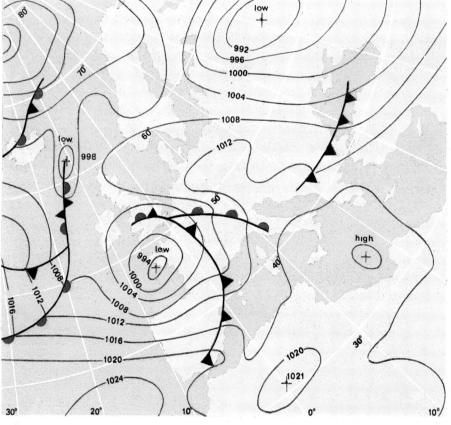

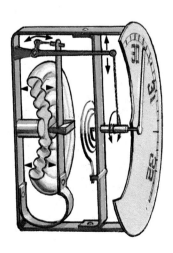

Metal box

47

Climates of the World

The climate is the average, or usual, weather of a place. Climates vary between the poles and the equator.

Climatic Regions

There are six main climatic regions. *Polar climates* are regions where the average temperature in the warmest month is less than 10°C. This is the climate of the frozen wastes around the poles and also the tundra, where the snow melts in summer.

Cold (coniferous) *forest* climates occur in a zone that stretches across North America and Eurasia. The average temperature in the coldest month is less than −3°C. But in the warmest month, the average temperature is above 10°C.

Temperate climates have an average temperature in the coldest month of not less than −3°C, but not more than 18°C. This climate includes mixed forest, deciduous forest and Mediterranean regions.

In *dry climates*, the total average yearly rainfall is less than 10 inches. Deserts may be hot or cold.

Tropical rainy climates have average temperatures in every month that are higher than 18°C. Some places have rain throughout the year. Others have one or two marked dry seasons.

Mountain climates vary as one climbs upwards, because temperatures fall with height. Some mountains on the equator have tropical climates at the bottom and polar climates at their snow-capped tops.

Above: Dense rain forests flourish in tropical rainy climates, where high temperatures and abundant rainfall encourage plant growth. The thickest forests are in regions which have rain throughout the year. Less dense forests grow in monsoon regions which have a marked dry season.

Left: In hot deserts, the only places with water are oases. Many oases are springs or wells which get water from the rocks below. Palm trees grow around them and camels can get much-needed water.

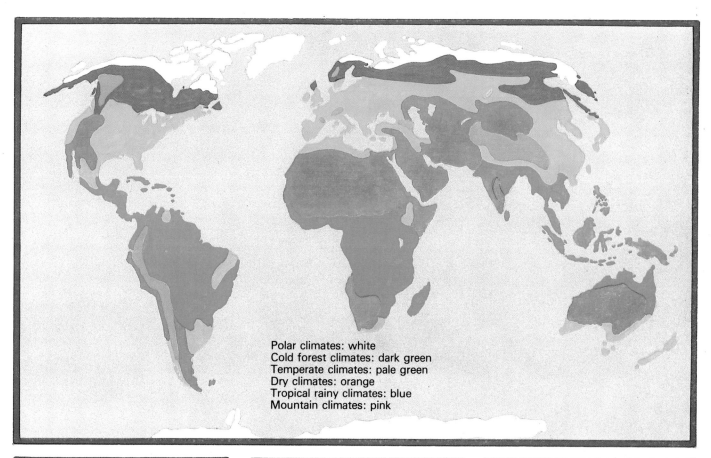

Polar climates: white
Cold forest climates: dark green
Temperate climates: pale green
Dry climates: orange
Tropical rainy climates: blue
Mountain climates: pink

Above: Vast coniferous forests, called taiga, grow in the northern hemisphere in the cold region between the temperate lands to the south and the tree-line, the northernmost limit of tree growth. Birds such as this capercaillie are quite common, though compared with other forests there are few plant and animal species.

Above: The temperate regions of the world were once covered by deciduous trees, which shed their leaves in winter. But most of the trees have now been cut down and replaced by farmland.

Top: The map shows the major climatic regions of the world.

Above: Around the poles, ice and snow blanket the land all the year round. But in the northern hemisphere, between the lands of permanent ice and the tree-line, is a zone called the tundra. This zone comes alive during the short, warm summer when the snow melts. Animal migrants such as musk-oxen and reindeer graze on the tundra. And the arctic fox's white coat turns red during the short summer months.

The Sea in Motion

The oceans cover about 71 per cent of the Earth's surface. Ocean water is always moving, even in the deepest trenches. We know this because fishes live there. If the water was still, the oxygen dissolved in the water would have been used up long ago.

Winds and Waves

Waves appear to move seawater. In fact, they make water particles rotate, but do not move them forwards. Most waves are caused by winds. Tsunamis are waves generated by earthquakes. These low but fast-moving waves often pass unnoticed in the open sea. But near land, they build up to great heights. A tsunami off Japan reached a height of 278 feet.

High Tide, Low Tide

Tides are caused by the gravitational pull of the Moon and, to a lesser extent, of the Sun. They occur twice every 24 hours and 50 minutes. This is the time taken by the Moon to complete one orbit of the Earth.

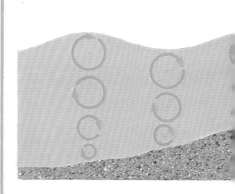

Above: When a wave passes through water, the particles of water rotate in a circular motion, but they are not moved sideways. The wave length is the distance between the crests of two successive waves. Along coasts, there is not enough water to complete the wave and so the wave breaks.

Ships caught at sea during a bad storm run the risk of capsizing. The highest waves in the open sea are caused by strong winds. The highest recorded wave measured 100 feet between the trough and the crest.

Rivers in the Sea

Sailors are interested in ocean currents, because they affect navigation. These currents, which are caused mainly by prevailing winds, only affect the top 1000 feet. Other currents lower down often move in an opposite direction to those on the surface. Many deep-sea currents are caused by variations in the density of the water. These result from differences in salinity (saltness) and temperature. Salty, cold water is denser (heavier) than less salty, warm water.

The circulation of ocean water by currents has an important effect on climate. Warm currents convey heat to cool temperate and polar regions. Cold currents also modify the climate of tropical regions.

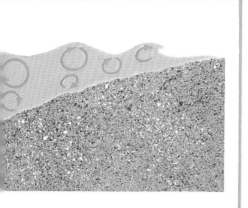

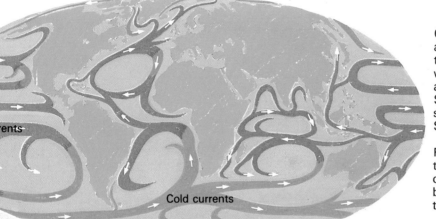

Warm currents

Cold currents

OCEAN CURRENTS

Ocean currents ensure that seawater is always on the move. The currents on the map (left) are caused mainly by winds. Ocean currents flow at 1-5 knots and so are important in navigation. Slower currents are called drifts. The slow northern extension of the fast Gulf Stream is the North Altantic Drift.

Other currents flow at lower levels. For example, warm currents flow towards the polar regions. There, denser (heavier) cold polar water sinks beneath the warm water and flows towards the equator.

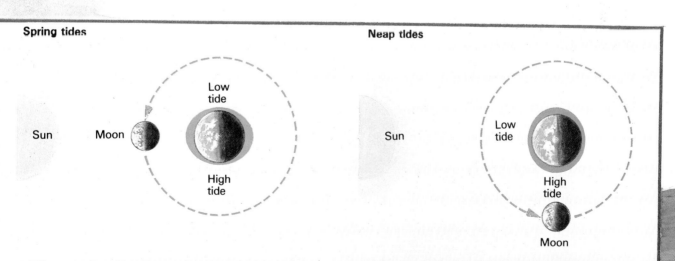

Spring tides

Sun   Moon

Low tide

High tide

Neap tides

Sun

Low tide

High tide

Moon

Tides are caused by the gravitational pull of the Moon and the Sun on the waters of the oceans. The highest tides are called spring tides. They occur when the Sun, Moon and Earth are in a straight line (above). The Moon's and the Sun's gravity are then combined.

The lowest tides are called neap tides. They occur when the Sun, Earth and Moon form a right angle (as shown above). The gravitational pull of the Moon is then opposed by the Sun's gravitational pull. Neap and spring tides each occur twice every month.

The Ocean Deeps

There are four oceans. The largest is the Pacific Ocean which covers about 64,000,000 sq. miles. This is about one third of the Earth's surface. The other oceans, in order of size, are the Atlantic, Indian and Arctic oceans.

Continental Shelves

Around land masses are gently sloping areas covered by shallow seas. These areas are called continental shelves. In places, such as western South America, the continental shelf is narrow. But off Land's End, England, the continental shelf extends 200 miles to the west. Continental shelves are flooded parts of the continents. They end at the steep continental slopes which plunge down to the abyss, the deep part of the ocean. The tops of the continental slopes are the true edges of the continents.

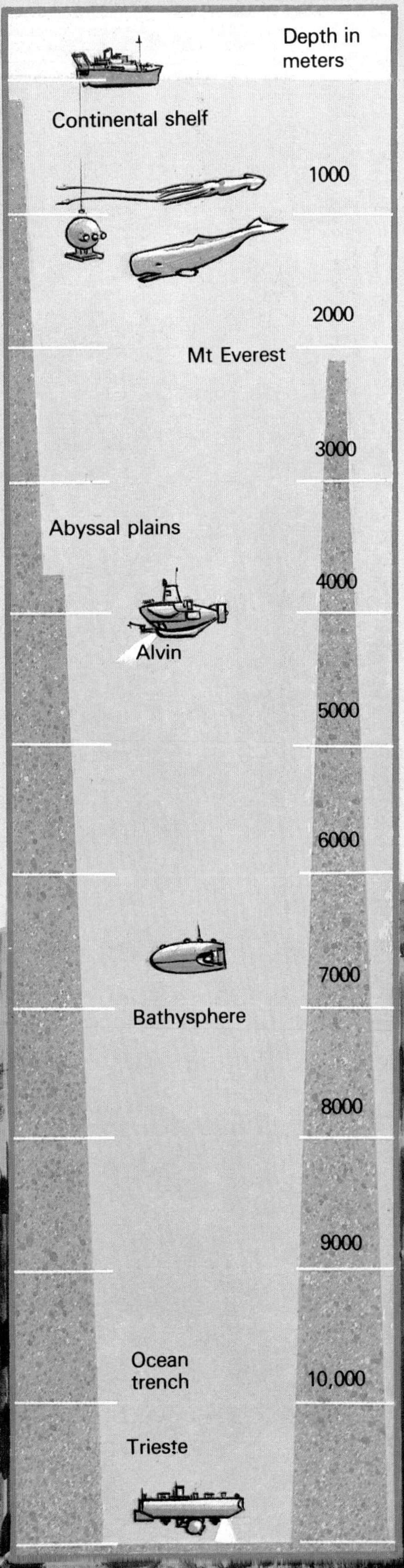

Left: If Mount Everest were placed in the deepest ocean trench, its peak would be about 6900 feet (2100 meters) below sea-level. The diagram also shows the depths reached by various manned submersibles.

Depth in meters

Continental shelf

1000

2000

Mt Everest

3000

Abyssal plains

4000

Alvin

5000

6000

7000

Bathysphere

8000

9000

Ocean trench

10,000

Trieste

The Abyss

The abyss was once thought to be a mostly flat plain covered by oozes. But mapping has shown that it contains several striking features.

The ocean trenches are the deepest parts of the oceans. The Mariana Trench reaches a depth of 36,198 feet (11,033 meters). The trenches are places where one plate is descending under another. As it descends, it melts (see pages 16-17). As a result, volcanic islands are found alongside the trenches. They get magma from the melting plates.

The ocean ridges are huge, long mountain ranges. Here, plates are moving apart and new crustal rock is being formed. Some volcanoes rise from the ocean ridges. Other volcanoes develop above isolated 'hot spots' in the Earth's mantle. Some volcanoes reach the surface as islands.

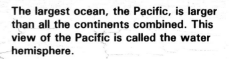

The largest ocean, the Pacific, is larger than all the continents combined. This view of the Pacific is called the water hemisphere.

Below: The diagram shows the main features of the oceans: the shallow continental shelves; the steep continental slopes; ocean trenches; volcanic mountains and islands; and long oceanic ridges.

Industry

Industry Around the World
In the last 200 years, the economies of many countries have changed, as farming and small-scale craft industries have become less important than mining and large-scale factory production. Such countries have been *industrialized*. The Industrial Revolution began in Britain in the late 18th century and Belgium, France, Germany and the USA soon followed. In the late 19th century, other countries, such as Canada, Japan, Russia and Sweden also began to industrialize.

The Pattern of Industry
The industrialized world now includes most of North America, Europe, the USSR, Japan, Australia and New Zealand. But most of Central and South America,

Africa and Asia have not been industrialized, although some countries, such as Brazil and China, already have sizeable industries which are expected to expand rapidly in the near future. Many poor countries would like to industrialize, but they lack the money and skilled workers needed to found industries.

Light and Heavy Industry
Light industry produces a wide range of goods, which are generally smaller than those produced by heavy industry. For example, the many consumer products which we find in supermarkets, including clothes, foods and household goods, are produced by light industries. Light industries are now changing because of the introduc-

tion of computers and automation.

Heavy industry is associated with huge factories, which use bulky raw materials to produce heavy products. Examples include the iron and steel industry, the chemical industry and heavy engineering, such as shipbuilding. Heavy industries were once located on coal- or iron-fields, because this reduced the cost of transporting these heavy raw materials. But many industries which use oil have spread to other areas in recent years. This is because oil is easily transported through pipelines.

Some industries are neither light nor heavy. For example, automobile assembly and aerospace industries combine elements from both.

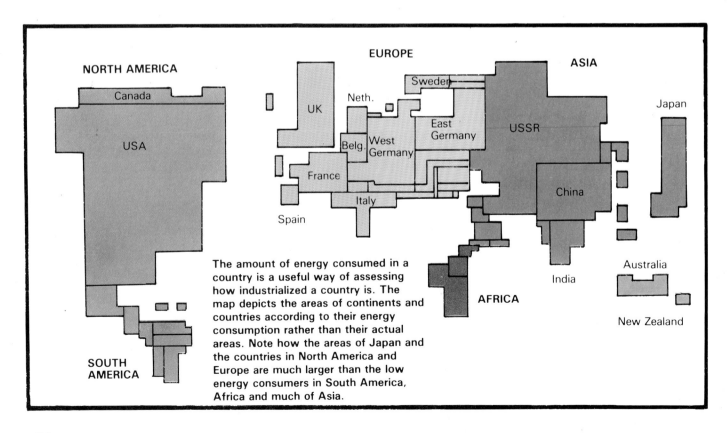

The amount of energy consumed in a country is a useful way of assessing how industrialized a country is. The map depicts the areas of continents and countries according to their energy consumption rather than their actual areas. Note how the areas of Japan and the countries in North America and Europe are much larger than the low energy consumers in South America, Africa and much of Asia.

Steel is the most important material used in shipbuilding, one of the world's leading heavy industries. In recent years, shipbuilders have made larger ships, including vast oil tankers, which can carry large amounts of bulk freight. Europe was once the main center of shipbuilding. But by the early 1980's Japan led the world, producing 48% of the world's merchant vessels, with North Korea accounting for another 9%. Following these two Asian countries were West Germany, Spain, Britain and Brazil.

Energy and Power

Manufacturing industry depends on a supply of cheap electrical energy. And we all take for granted that we can heat and light our homes at the turn of a switch. Energy is produced in several ways.

Fossil Fuels
Most of the world's energy is produced by oil, natural gas and coal. These fossil fuels are made of the remains of once-living plants and animals.

Oil and gas often collect, as shown in the diagram below, in upfolds of porous rocks, through which gases and liquids can flow. Above and below are impervious rocks which block the flow of gas and liquids. The gas and oil collect at the top of the upfold. Beneath the oil, the porous rock is often filled with water.

Coal is generally more expensive to mine and, by weight, it gives out less heat than oil and gas. But it is valuable in industry and coal production has remained roughly the same over the last 30 years.

Fossil fuels are being used up at a faster rate than they are being renewed naturally. As a result, they will eventually run out. Scientists are, therefore, looking for other ways of producing energy.

Petroleum is fairly easy to extract and to transport through pipelines. Below: Oil is often trapped in anticlines (upfolds) of porous rock layers.

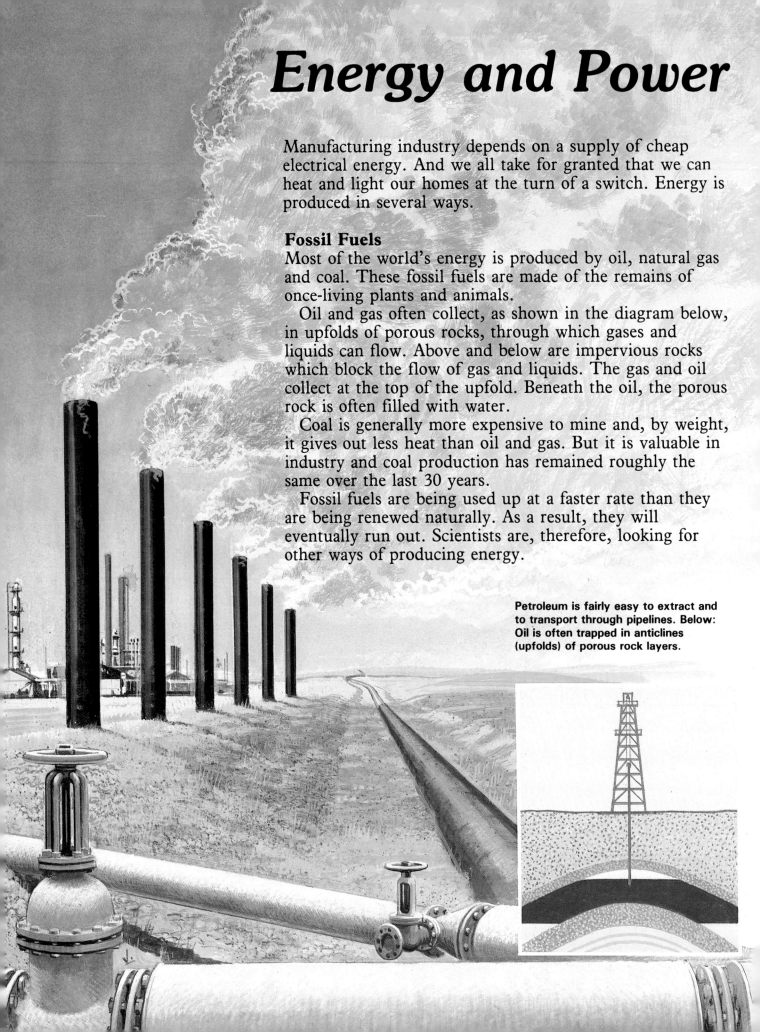

ENERGY PRODUCTION

COAL Leading coal producers in 1981 were: USA (25.4% of world output); China (21.9%), the USSR (18.6%), Poland (5.9%), South Africa (4.8%) and the UK (4.6%).

OIL Leading producers in 1983 were: USSR (22.4%), USA (17.7%), Saudi Arabia (8.9%), Mexico (5.4%), Iran (4.5%) and the UK (4.1%).

NATURAL GAS Major producers in 1981 were the USA (29.9%), USSR (23.2%), Canada (3.9%), the Netherlands (3.8%), and the UK (2.1%).

HYDROELECTRICITY 99% of Norway's electricity supply comes from hydroelectric stations, 92% in Brazil and 70% in Canada.

NUCLEAR POWER stations supply 40% of France's electricity, 37% of Sweden's and 36% of Finland's.

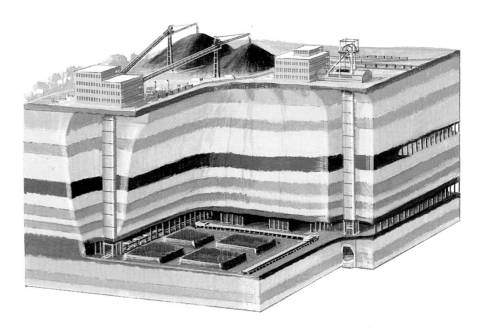

Above: The diagram shows an underground coal mine. Shafts are used to ventilate the mine and also to extract stale air. The coal is cut with modern machines. It is then transported to the upcast shaft where it is raised to the surface.

Other Sources of Energy

Some electrical energy comes from hydroelectric power stations. The cost of building dams and generating stations is high, but production costs are low and it does not cause pollution. Nuclear, or atomic, energy is also important, but some people are worried about the dangers involved in getting rid of nuclear wastes.

Other methods include improved windmills and solar power stations which use concentrated sunlight to heat water. In some areas, water from hot springs and geysers is used. Water can be heated by pumping it far into the ground. If this water was pumped back to the surface, it could be used to run generators.

Below: The chart shows the sources of world energy consumption. Oil is the chief fossil fuel, followed by coal and natural gas.

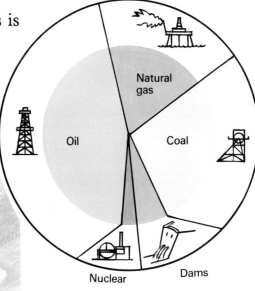

Left: In wet countries with plenty of steep slopes, such as Norway, rivers are dammed. The water in the man-made reservoirs is used to turn turbines which drive the generators that produce electric power for homes and factories.

Forestry

Wood is a valuable product. It is used in building, for furniture and in making paper. It also has many less obvious uses, as in the manufacture of such things as explosives, manmade fibers and medicines.

Forests cover about one-third of the world's surface. The *coniferous* (evergreen) *forests* are most widespread in the northern hemisphere. They contain cedars, firs, pines and spruces that are adapted to survive long, cold winters. These commercially valuable trees are also called *softwoods*, because most, though not all, species are easy to saw. The leading softwood producers are the USSR, the USA and Canada.

Temperate hardwood forests contain such deciduous trees as ash, beech, chestnut, elm, hickory, oak and willow,

In North America, northern Europe and the USSR, forestry is highly mechanized. Lumberjacks fell trees with powersaws and felling machines. Many of the trunks are transported from the logging camps to rivers, where they are floated downstream to a sawmill. Some heavy hardwoods will not float. They must be transported by road or rail.

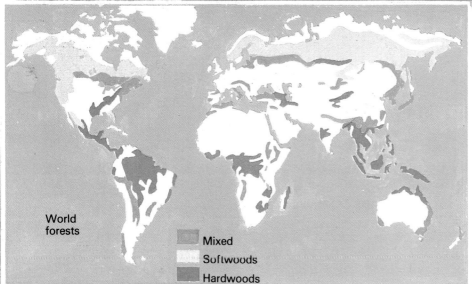

World forests

Mixed
Softwoods
Hardwoods

Above: The most valuable tropical hardwoods are usually scattered throughout the dense forests. This makes their extraction difficult. In southern Asia elephants are often used to drag the tree trunks through the forest to rivers or loading sites.

Left: The map shows that the world's main softwood forests are in the northern hemisphere — in North America, Scandinavia and the USSR. In some areas, these forests merge southwards into mixed forests and, eventually, deciduous (hardwood) forests. The largest hardwood forests, however, are in the tropics, especially the Amazon basin, central Africa and South-East Asia.

which shed their leaves in autumn. A third type of forest is the *mixed forest* zone between the coniferous and hardwood forests. The fourth type of forest, the tropical hardwood forest, contains such trees as ebony, mahogany, rosewood and teak.

Foresters in the northern coniferous forests carefully replace the trees they cut down with young saplings grown from seed in tree nurseries. However, in recent years, acid rain has been killing many trees. Acid rain is formed when raindrops dissolve harmful gases emitted from factories and power stations.

The huge tropical hardwood forests are being destroyed even faster. In the early 1980s, an area of tropical forest the size of Scotland was being cut down every year. If this continues, there will be no tropical forest left in 40 years.

Farming Round the World

Some countries are densely populated, but have only a small area of flat farmland. They build terraces, like a series of steps, down hillsides. The walls around the terraces stop rainwater running downwards washing away the soil.

The world's chief farming nations are China, the USSR, the USA and India. But their farming industries differ greatly. In the USSR and the USA, farmers use modern machinery and yields are high. In China and India, much of the work is done by hand and yields are lower.

There are two main types of farming. Arable farming is the growing of crops. Pastoral farming is the production of meat and other animal products.

Tropical Farming

Many farmers in the tropics are poor, producing only enough food for their families. This is subsistence farming. Some farmers move every few years, whenever the fertility of their farms is exhausted. Nomadic pastoralists wander around with their animals. These simple forms of farming contrast with tropical plantation agriculture, which uses scientific methods to produce such cash crops as cocoa, coffee and tea.

THE INVENTION OF FARMING

Farming was invented about 10,000 years ago, when people learned how to plant seeds. The earliest known farms were in south-western Asia, but farming began soon afterwards in many other parts of the world. In a short time, most people gave up the old hunting and gathering way of life and settled down to become farmers. The farmers founded the first villages and towns.

In the Nile valley in Egypt, in the Tigris and Euphrates valleys in what is now Iraq, and in the Indus valley of Pakistan, people learned how to irrigate the valleys by moving water from the rivers to their fields. From about 5000 years ago, these valleys became centers of brilliant early civilizations.

WORKING ON FARMS

The farming industry in developed countries is highly mechanized and so it employs few people. Examples, with the percentages of people employed on farms, are as follows:

USA	2%	Britian	2%
Belgium	3%	West Germany	4%
Canada	5%	Australia	6%

By contrast, the farming industry is the chief employer in developing countries. For example:

Chad	85%	Tanzania	83%
Ethiopia	80%	Afghanistan	79%
India	71%	China	69%

Farming in Temperate Lands

Farms near cities in temperate countries produce fresh food for city-dwellers. These farms are called truck farms or market gardens. This is a type of intensive farming. Intensive farming is important in densely populated countries. By contrast, ranching is a kind of extensive farming. Extensive farms are usually on land which is unsuitable for intensive crop growing. Another type of farming is called mixed farming. Mixed farms produce crops and animal products.

Working Together

In some countries, groups of farmers choose to work together through co-operatives. Collective farms in many Communist countries are similar except that people were forced to join them. On collectives, farmers work together and share the produce. They do not receive wages like the workers on the USSR's *sovkhozy* (government-owned farms).

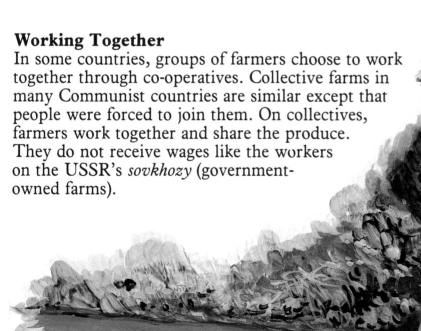

Harvest of the Sea

Fish is a valuable food. In some countries, including Japan and Norway, it makes up about one-tenth of people's diets. Freshwater fish form about one-tenth of the world's total catch of 75 million tons. The richest ocean fishing grounds are in the north-western Pacific Ocean and in the north-eastern Atlantic Ocean. More fish are caught in the shallow waters of the continental shelves than in the deep ocean waters.

Traditionally, fishermen were hunters, who were never sure of a good catch. Today, however, modern technology is aiding fishermen. For example, radar and sonic depth finders are used to locate shoals of fish.

The use of modern methods has led to overfishing in some areas. This has led to a search for new food products from the oceans. For example, krill, a shrimp-like creature, is found in great quantities in the waters around Antarctica. If ways can be found to package it attractively, it may become a food for people. It could also become a major animal food.

WHALING

Whaling is an ancient industry. The chief products are oil, meat for human and animal consumption, whale bones and ambergris, a waxy substance found in the intestines of some sperm whales, which is used to fix odors in expensive perfumes.

The chief whaling countries are Japan, the USSR, the Faroe Islands (Denmark) and Norway. About three-quarters of the catch is processed on large factory ships, which get their whales from small catcher boats equipped with harpoon guns.

Whaling has brought some whale species close to extinction. For example, the seas around Antarctica contained about 14,500 blue whales (the world's largest animal) in the 1930s. By 1968, there were only 600 left. Today, international treaties ban the hunting of many species.

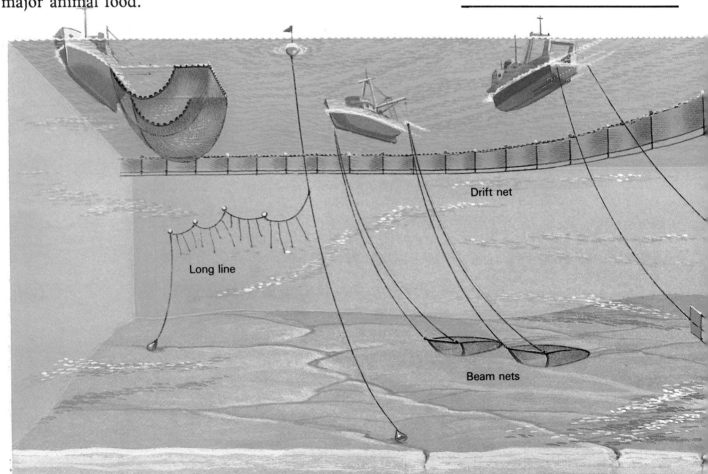

Long line

Drift net

Beam nets

Fish Farming

Attempts are now being made to conserve fish and to develop fish farms. The breeding and raising of fish in tanks and ponds is called aquaculture. Carp have been raised in China for thousands of years, and oysters have been bred in Europe since Roman times.

Today, many species of freshwater fish, including carp, eels and trout are successfully raised. And young salmon are reared in fresh water and later moved to salt water. This mimics the conditions experienced by wild salmon which migrate from rivers to the oceans. The farming of saltwater fish is generally less economic, but overfishing in the oceans is making scientists study saltwater fish farming.

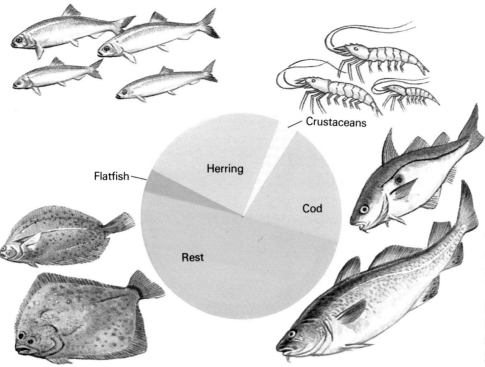

Above: The diagram shows the proportions of various fishes and crustaceans caught around the world. The chief fishing nation is Japan. It accounts for about one-seventh of the world's total catch.

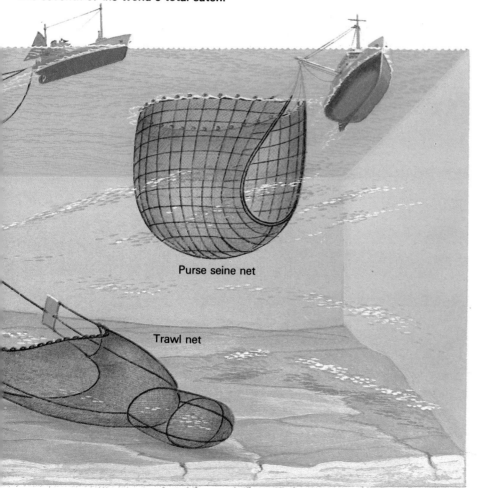

Left: The diagram shows various techniques used in the fishing industry. Long-lining involves putting out long, or ground, lines. Attached to them are short lines with baited hooks. This technique is used to catch tuna.

Drift or gill nets are held up by floats. The gills of fish which try to swim through the nets are caught in the mesh. Many herrings and mackerel are caught by drift nets.

Drag or trawl nets are large, bag-shaped nets which are dragged along the seabed at depths as great as 3000 feet. These nets are used to catch flatfish and other bottom-living fish and crustaceans.

Purse seine nets are used when shoals of such fishes as sardines and herrings are located on the ship's radar. The purse seine nets are then drawn around the shoal.

Pacific shrimp boats haul two beam nets across the sea floor. They catch prawns and shrimps. Many catcher boats now work with a mother factory ship. Instead of returning to port, they deliver their catch to a large factory ship. There the fish are rapidly processed and frozen.

Peoples of the World

People belong to the species *Homo sapiens* (intelligent man). They first appeared around 50,000 years ago. They displaced the closely related Neanderthal people, who died out around the end of the Ice Age.

People vary in appearance. Many of these differences are probably adaptations to the varied climatic conditions in which the people developed. The human family is divided into four main sub-groups: Caucasoids, Mongoloids, Negroids and Australoids.

Caucasoids include the mostly fair-skinned people of Europe and the many people of European origin in other continents. The Arabs of North Africa and most of the much darker skinned people of north-eastern Africa, south-western Asia and India are also Caucasoids.

Mongoloids, with the yellowish skin and straight, dark hair, include most of the people of eastern Asia, Eskimos and American Indians. Negroids include the Black people of Africa and Black Americans, the descendants of Black African slaves.

Australoids include Australian Aborigines, the Veddoids of southern India and the Ainu, the first inhabitants of Japan.

Below: Examples of members of the human family. Most Europeans, Arabs and most people in south-western Asia and India are Caucasoids. Australian Aborigines belong to the Australoid sub-group. The Negroid group includes Black Africans and Black Americans. The Mongoloid sub-group includes most people in eastern Asia and the American Indians. Members of the sub-groups have intermarried. For example, many Mexicans are mestizos, of mixed European and American Indian descent.

Above: The first North Americans came from Asia, perhaps 40,000 years ago, during the Ice Age. The sea level was then much lower than it is today and a land bridge connected northern Asia and North America. These Mongoloid people were the ancestors of the American Indians.

Ways of Life

The ways of life of people still vary greatly around the world. There are still a few people, including the Bushmen and pygmies of Africa, who live much like our ancestors before the invention of agriculture. They live by hunting animals and gathering seeds and roots. Other people are farmers, though many farmers in Africa, Asia and South America are poor. But more and more people are making their homes in cities and towns. The chief jobs in the developed western countries are in manufacturing and service industries.

Religions of the World

People differ in many ways. For example, religion divides many people. The world's main religions — Hinduism, Buddhism, Shintoism, Taoism, Confucianism, Christianity and Islam — all originated in Asia. The greatest number of people now belong to the various Christian churches. Of the more than 1000 million Christians, 73 per cent are Roman Catholics.

LANGUAGES

There are about 3000 languages and many more dialects. Many have large vocabularies and a written form. Others contain comparatively few words and have no written form.

Some languages are closely related to each other. French, Italian, Portuguese and Spanish all come from Latin, the language of ancient Rome. These languages form the Romance language group. This group belongs to a wider family of languages, called the Indo-European family. This is the world's largest family, followed by the Sino-Tibetan, which includes Chinese.

Some languages have spread around the world. The chief international language is English. French, German and Spanish are also spoken widely throughout the world.

Towns and Cities

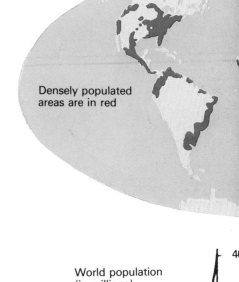

Densely populated areas are in red

The world's population has steadily increased through human history and farmers have had to produce more and more food every year. In the late 1970s, the yearly rate of increase was 1.7 per cent, but there were signs that the rate was slowing. In some developed countries, populations were staying the same or even declining. But in many poor countries, the rates were still increasing. For example, Africa's population was increasing by 2.9 per cent a year, as compared with 0.4 per cent in Europe. Overall, the world's population is expected to continue growing until about AD 2100, when it will level out at around 10,200 million, as compared with 4800 million in 1985.

More and more people are living in cities and towns. For instance, 91 per cent of Britons live in urban areas. In poor countries, where most people are farmers, urban populations are much smaller. But even there, cities are growing quickly. Many do not have enough houses or jobs for their fast-increasing populations. Many people, therefore, are forced to live in unhealthy slums on the outskirts of cities.

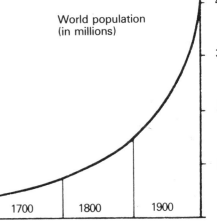

World population (in millions)

| AD 1000 | 1100 | 1200 | 1300 | 1400 | 1500 | 1600 | 1700 | 1800 | 1900 |

1

2

3

Above: The reasons why the sites of many ancient cities were chosen were concerned with trade or defense. Some lay on easy river crossings (2), where trade routes naturally converged. Other trading cities grew up around sheltered harbors (1). Some cities were centers of government, while others developed around military outposts, such as castles (3).

Below: Cities are growing throughout the world. For example, in Brazil, 45 out of every 100 people lived in urban areas in 1960, as compared with 69 in 1982. People are attracted by services and jobs which rural areas lack. But many cities have grown so rapidly that newcomers cannot find jobs. They live in shanty towns.

Above: The map shows that the world's population is unevenly distributed. Large areas near the poles, in mountains and in deserts are almost empty of people.

Left: The graph shows how the world's population has increased from AD 1000, when it stood at about 300 million, to the present day. It shows that the rate of population has been steadily accelerating. The world's population passed the 1000 million mark in the 19th century, 2000 million in the 1920s and 4000 million in the mid-1970s.

Rich and Poor

Our world is divided into the rich 'haves' and the poor 'have-nots'. In rich western countries, people have an average life expectancy at birth of more than 70 years. But in much of Africa and Asia people, on average, do not live much beyond 50 years.

The economies of most African and Asian countries are underdeveloped, or 'developing'. Most people are farmers and there is little manufacturing. Also, the countries' minerals are mostly exported to the rich countries. Many people have poor diets and many starve when the crops fail, after droughts or floods.

The rich, developed and industrialized countries give aid to developing countries. But this aid is often insufficient, especially because the populations of most developing nations are increasing rapidly.

Many poor countries want to set up industries, but this is expensive. Other countries are trying to develop agriculture. This wide gap between rich and poor nations, which in many cases is widening, is one of the most serious problems facing us all.

OUR DIVIDED WORLD

Developing countries include four main subgroups:

LOW INCOME ECONOMIES
These, the poorest countries, are found mainly in Africa and Asia. They include Chad, Ethiopia, India, Pakistan and Zaire.

MIDDLE INCOME OIL EXPORTERS
These are somewhat wealthier countries, largely because they export oil. They include Algeria, Mexico, Nigeria and Venezuela.

OTHER MIDDLE INCOME ECONOMIES
Some of these countries have begun to industrialize their economies. They include Argentina and Brazil.

HIGH INCOME OIL EXPORTERS
These include the oil-rich countries of the Arabian peninsula.

DEVELOPED COUNTRIES
The developed, industrialized world includes most of West Europe, the USA and Canada, Australia and New Zealand, and Japan. The East European countries and the USSR are regarded as a separate group.

Right: The map shows the world divided according to countries' per capita gross domestic products (the value of the goods and services created by each person in one year). This is a measure of a country's wealth.

Below: India is a poor country, with a per capita gross domestic product in 1982 of $210, as compared with $13,000 in the USA. Many city-dwellers in India are poor but the villagers are even poorer. The inset picture shows the contrast in the developed world where many people have money left over after they have paid for the essentials of life to spend on consumer products such as cars and even yachts.

Over $10,000 per person
$5000-10,000 per person
$1000-5000 per person
$500-1000 per person
Under $500 per person

Transport and Trade

The richer countries have well organized transport systems. This is because the easy, rapid and cheap movement of goods is essential for their economies. By contrast, many poor countries lack good transport systems. This lack hampers their development.

In developed countries, railroads became the chief form of land transport in the early days of the Industrial Revolution. But in recent times, road haulage has proved a cheaper and faster means of transport. Yet it is still easier to move bulky, heavy goods by rail or inland waterways, though oil, a fluid, is most easily moved by pipelines.

Oil is also transported by ocean-going tankers. In recent years, larger and larger ships have been built for carrying freight. Also, the use of large boxes, called containers, has speeded up the handling of goods at ports. Air transport is expensive, but it is suitable for light and costly goods.

The Trading Nations

World trade is concerned with the buying (or importing) and selling (or exporting) of raw materials, including food, manufactures and services. The leading trading nations, including the USA, West Germany, Japan, France and Britain, are all developed nations. The total value of the trade of developing nations is much smaller. They mostly export raw materials and import manufactured goods.

Trade helps to develop the economies of countries and raise people's living standards. To encourage trade, many countries work together through regional organizations, such as the European Economic Community (sometimes known as the Common Market). This organization was set up in 1958 by Belgium, France, West Germany, Italy, Luxembourg and the Netherlands. By the end of 1984 the original six countries had been joined by Denmark, the Republic of Ireland and the United Kingdom.

Left: Oil is one of the most important items in world trade. It is transported across land through long pipelines and across the oceans in huge oil tankers. The tankers deliver the oil to manufacturers who use it as a fuel, a lubricant and as a raw material in the chemical industry.

Right: The earliest form of transport was human labor, but domesticated animals proved much more efficient. Until about 150 years ago, beasts of burden were the chief means of moving goods. Camels are still important in desert regions. These sturdy animals can go several days without water.

In poor countries, farmers take any spare food or other goods to open-air markets in towns and cities. Some farmers travel down rivers and they use their boats as floating shops in river markets. People once bartered (exchanged) goods for other goods. But most people now use money for buying and selling.

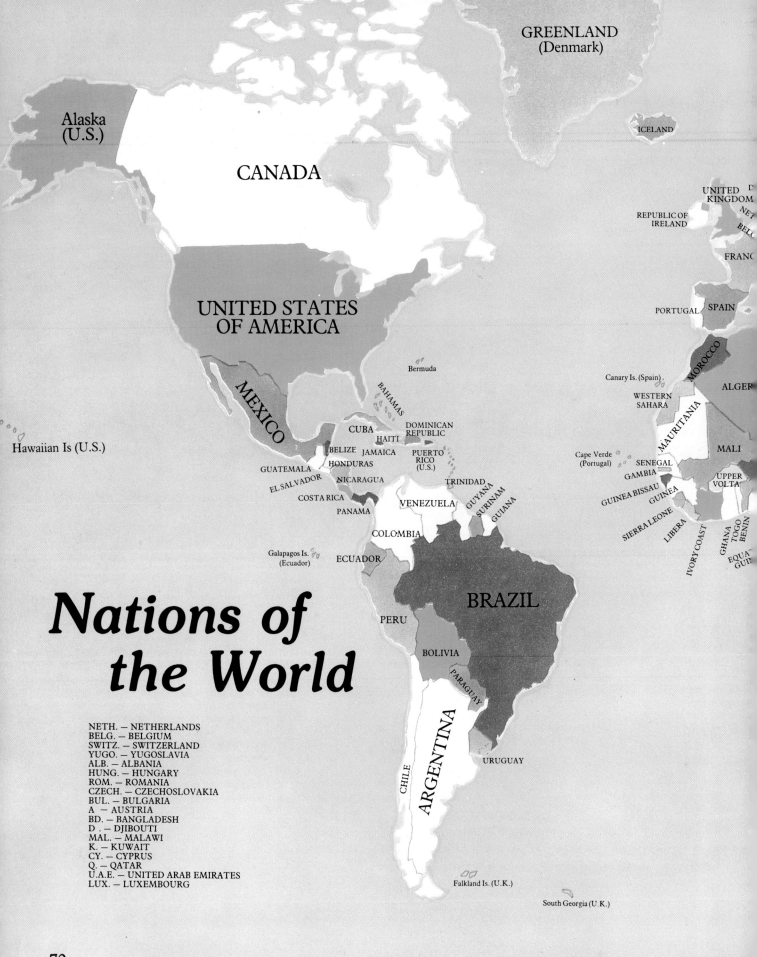

GREENLAND
(Denmark)

Alaska
(U.S.)

CANADA

ICELAND

UNITED
KINGDOM

REPUBLIC OF
IRELAND

NET

BELG

FRANC

UNITED STATES
OF AMERICA

PORTUGAL

SPAIN

MOROCCO

ALGER

MEXICO

Bermuda

Canary Is. (Spain)

WESTERN
SAHARA

MAURITANIA

MALI

Hawaiian Is (U.S.)

BAHAMAS

CUBA

DOMINICAN
REPUBLIC

HAITI

BELIZE

JAMAICA

PUERTO
RICO
(U.S.)

Cape Verde
(Portugal)

SENEGAL

GAMBIA

UPPER
VOLTA

GUATEMALA

HONDURAS

EL SALVADOR

NICARAGUA

TRINIDAD

GUINEA BISSAU

GUINEA

COSTA RICA

VENEZUELA

GUYANA

SURINAM

SIERRA LEONE

LIBERA

IVORY COAST

GHANA

TOGO

BENIN

PANAMA

COLOMBIA

GUIANA

EQUA.
GUIN

Galapagos Is.
(Ecuador)

ECUADOR

Nations of
the World

PERU

BRAZIL

BOLIVIA

PARAGUAY

NETH. — NETHERLANDS
BELG. — BELGIUM
SWITZ. — SWITZERLAND
YUGO. — YUGOSLAVIA
ALB. — ALBANIA
HUNG. — HUNGARY
ROM. — ROMANIA
CZECH. — CZECHOSLOVAKIA
BUL. — BULGARIA
A — AUSTRIA
BD. — BANGLADESH
D . — DJIBOUTI
MAL. — MALAWI
K. — KUWAIT
CY. — CYPRUS
Q. — QATAR
U.A.E. — UNITED ARAB EMIRATES
LUX. — LUXEMBOURG

CHILE

ARGENTINA

URUGUAY

Falkland Is. (U.K.)

South Georgia (U.K.)

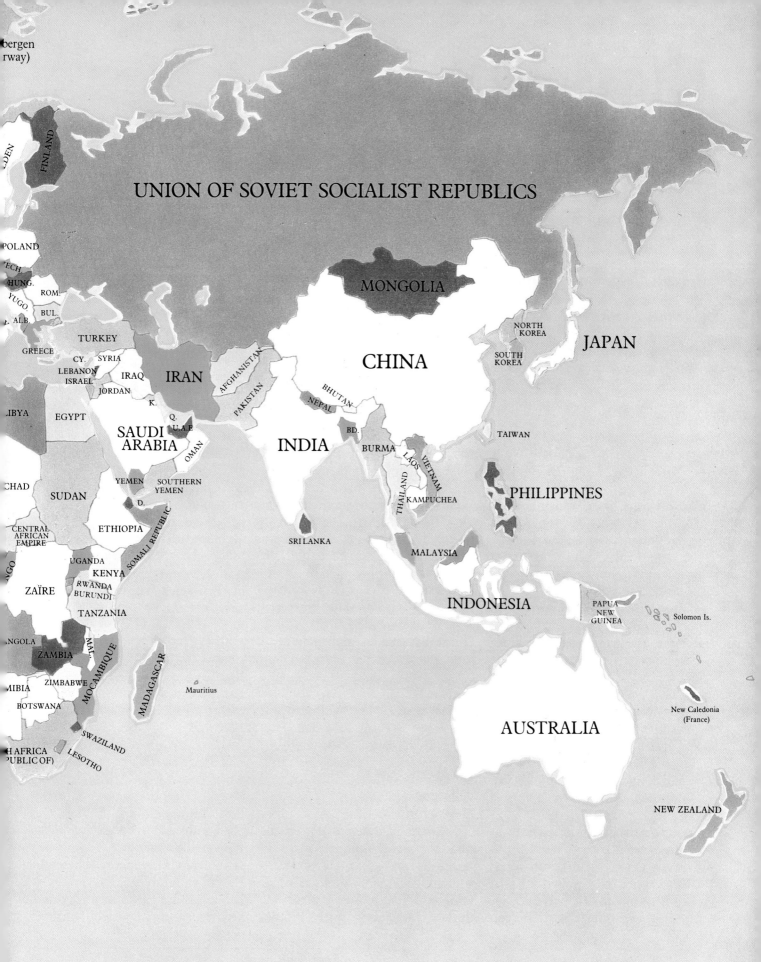

(bergen
rway)

SDEN

FINLAND

UNION OF SOVIET SOCIALIST REPUBLICS

POLAND

ECH

HUNG.

ROM.

YUGO.

L. ALB.

BUL.

TURKEY

GREECE

CY.

SYRIA

LEBANON

ISRAEL

JORDAN

IRAQ

IRAN

AFGHANISTAN

PAKISTAN

MONGOLIA

NORTH
KOREA

SOUTH
KOREA

JAPAN

CHINA

BHUTAN

NEPAL

TAIWAN

LIBYA

EGYPT

SAUDI
ARABIA

K.

Q.

U.A.E.

OMAN

INDIA

BD.

BURMA

LAOS

VIETNAM

THAILAND

KAMPUCHEA

PHILIPPINES

CHAD

SUDAN

YEMEN

SOUTHERN
YEMEN

D.

ETHIOPIA

SRI LANKA

MALAYSIA

CENTRAL
AFRICAN
EMPIRE

NGO

UGANDA

KENYA

RWANDA

BURUNDI

SOMALI REPUBLIC

INDONESIA

PAPUA
NEW
GUINEA

Solomon Is.

ZAÏRE

TANZANIA

NGOLA

ZAMBIA

MAL.

MOCAMBIQUE

MADAGASCAR

Mauritius

New Caledonia
(France)

MIBIA

ZIMBABWE

BOTSWANA

SWAZILAND

AUSTRALIA

H AFRICA
PUBLIC OF)

LESOTHO

NEW ZEALAND

ANTARCTICA

73

Glossary

Aborigine The original inhabitant of a country, such as the Australian Aborigines.

Alluvium Sand, silt and mud, which are carried and deposited by rivers.

Ammonites A large group of molluscs, the fossils of which are common in Mesozoic rocks. At the end of this era, they became extinct.

Anemometer An instrument used to measure wind speeds. Some also show wind directions.

Anticyclone A region of high air pressure, where air is descending. It is associated with stable weather conditons.

Aquifer A layer of rock through which water can percolate. Wells are sunk down to aquifers in order to bring water to the surface.

Atoll A coral island which is often circular or horseshoe-shaped. It often contains a lagoon.

Aurorae Lights, called the Aurora Borealis in the northern hemisphere and the Aurora Australis in the southern, that appear in the skies in polar regions. They occur when streams of charged particles from the Sun collide with particles in the ionosphere. They include streamers of light, and red and green lights lasting several hours.

Beaufort scale A scale from 0 to 12 for classifying wind speeds.

Biogeography The study of the distribution of plants and animals.

Caldera A crater in the top of a volcano. Some contain lakes.

Campos Tropical grassland in South America.

Canyon A steep-sided river valley.

Cash crop A crop grown for sale, not for use by the farmer.

Cave A hollow in the Earth's crust. Caves on coasts are worn out by wave action, while lava caves are found in hardened lava flows. The largest caves occur in limestone and dolomite. They are the result of chemical weathering.

Condensation A change of state, as when a gas or vapor turns into a liquid. Condensation occurs in cooling air when invisible water vapor is turned into visible water droplets (clouds).

Continent A large landmass, including adjacent islands. The world's seven continents are, in order of size, Asia, Africa, North America, South America, Antarctica, Europe and Oceania.

Coriolis effect The deflection of winds and ocean currents caused by the rotation of the Earth on its axis. Winds and currents are deflected to the right of the direction in which they are moving in the northern hemisphere and to the left in the southern hemisphere.

Cyclone A low air pressure system. It is sometimes used to mean the same as a depression.

Delta An area at the mouth of some rivers that has been built up by sediment brought there by the river.

Depression A low pressure air system which forms along the polar front where warm air brought by westerlies meets up with cold air in the polar easterlies. It is associated with unsettled weather.

Developing country A country which is either poor or, as in the case of wealthy oil exporters in south-western Asia, a country which is only partly industrialized.

Dinosaur A term meaning 'terrible lizard'. Dinosaurs were reptiles which lived in the Mesozoic era.

Ecology The study of living things and how they are related to each other and to the environments in which they are found.

Evaporation A change of state, as when a liquid becomes a gas or a vapor.

Frost Frozen moisture on the Earth's surface formed when water vapor condenses in air that is below 0°C.

Galaxy A system containing millions of stars, such as the Milky Way galaxy to which our Solar System belongs.

Gross domestic product or **GDP** The total value of all the goods and services produced in a country in a given period of time. The annual per capita GDP is the GDP for a particular year divided by the population in that year.

Gross national product or **GNP** The gross domestic product, plus income from investments and possessions owned abroad, less income earned at home that goes to foreigners.

Hail Pellets of ice that fall from clouds.

Hemisphere Half a sphere. The Earth is divided by the equator into the northern and southern hemispheres.

Industrialization A change in the economy of a country which occurs when mining and manufacturing become more important than farming. Countries going through this change are said to be undergoing an Industrial Revolution.

Insolation The energy which the Earth gets from the Sun.

International date line A boundary around longitude 180 degrees

East or West, where there is a time difference of 24 hours. This is because time is measured east and west of Greenwich Mean Time (GMT). Going westwards from Greenwich, 180° represents a loss of 12 hours. Going eastwards, 180° represents a gain of 12 hours. This gives a time difference of 24 hours, or one whole day.

Ionosphere A layer of the atmosphere, which starts at about 80 km above the surface, and ends at about 500 km, where the exosphere begins. The air here is extremely thin. Most gas particles are ionized (electrically charged) by cosmic or solar rays. Aurorae occur in the ionosphere (see Aurorae).

Jet stream A strong wind that blows around the Earth from west to east near the top of the troposphere and in the lower stratosphere. They occur in the middle latitudes. Airline pilots use them as tail winds but avoid flying into them.

Life expectancy The average length of people's lives. In 1982, the life expectancy at birth ranged from about 36 years in Afghanistan to 79 years in Switzerland.

Llanos Tropical grassland in South America.

Map projection A means of representing the curved surface of the Earth on a flat sheet of paper. Most projections are devised by mathematical means.

Monsoon A wind system in which the prevailing wind direction is reversed from one season to another.

Moraine The loose rock carried by glaciers and ice sheets. *Lateral* moraine is carried on the sides of glaciers. Rock frozen in the ice is called *englacial* moraine and rock frozen in the base is *subglacial* moraine. Fragments dragged along under the ice are called *ground*

moraine. Moraine is dumped at the edge of the glacier or ice sheet to form various land features, such as ridges of *terminal moraine.*

Neanderthal Man A type of *Homo sapiens* which became extinct about 10,000 years ago.

Nomad A person who leads a wandering life, such as a hunter-gatherer or a livestock herder.

Oasis A place in a desert where there is water. Small oases occur around springs or wells. The Nile valley in north-eastern Africa is a large oasis.

Ozone A form of oxygen with three atoms in the molecule, rather than the usual two.

Pampas Temperate grassland in southern South America.

Parkland Grasslands in Australia.

Permafrost Permanently frozen subsoil in polar regions.

Prairie The grasslands of central North America.

Precipitation Any moisture caused by the condensation of water vapor in the air, including rain, snow, sleet, hail, frost and dew.

Pyroclasts Fragments of rock made of bits of magma which have been hurled out of volcanoes. They range in size from volcanic dust to large loaf-sized volcanic bombs.

Rainbow Arcs of colored light which occur when the Sun's rays are reflected and refracted by raindrops in the air. The colors are red, orange, yellow, green, blue, indigo and violet.

Rain gauge An instrument used to measure precipitation. It consists of an open funnel leading into a collecting jar.

Savanna Tropical grassland, often with scattered trees.

Scarp A steep slope formed by movements of rocks along faults, or by the erosion of gently tilted resistant rocks.

Selvas The dense rain forests in

the huge Amazon basin of South America.

Shifting cultivation A method of farming whereby people clear a patch of forest or other land and farm it until the soil loses its fertility. The people then move on to a new clearing. It is common in tropical regions.

Silt Fine rock grains carried by rivers. Silt is finer than sand, but coarser than mud.

Spring A flow of water from the rocks on to the surface. Many springs are the sources of rivers.

Steppe Grassland in south-east Europe and in the south-west USSR.

Synoptic chart A weather map that shows weather conditions over a large area at a particular time.

Transhumance The seasonal movement of livestock. In Switzerland, farmers keep their animals in the sheltered valleys in winter. In summer, they graze their animals on the lush mountain pastures.

Tropics The region between the Tropic of Cancer (latitude 23° 27′ North) and the Tropic of Capricorn (latitude 23° 27′ South).

Tundra The treeless region between the ice-covered polar regions and the coniferous forests (taiga).

Veld The high grasslands of South Africa.

Water cycle The process by which there is a constant interchange of water between the oceans and the continents.

Water table The level of ground water in the rocks beneath the Earth's surface.

Weather The day to day or hour to hour condition of the air.

Well A hole dug down to the water table so that water can be obtained.

Zoogeography The study of the distribution of animals, a branch of biogeography.

Index